FUNDAMENTAL ENGLISH AND MATHEMATICS SKILLS FOR TRAINEE TEACHERS

Sara Miller McCune founded SAGE Publishing in 1965 to support the dissemination of usable knowledge and educate a global community. SAGE publishes more than 1000 journals and over 800 new books each year, spanning a wide range of subject areas. Our growing selection of library products includes archives, data, case studies and video. SAGE remains majority owned by our founder and after her lifetime will become owned by a charitable trust that secures the company's continued independence.

Los Angeles | London | New Delhi | Singapore | Washington DC | Melbourne

FUNDAMENTAL ENGLISH AND MATHEMATICS SKILLS FOR TRAINEE TEACHERS

MARK PATMORE, SARAH WOODHOUSE
REBECCA PETRONZI AND CHARLOTTE MOSEY

Learning Matters
A SAGE Publishing Company
1 Oliver's Yard
55 City Road
London EC1Y 1SP

SAGE Publications Inc.
2455 Teller Road
Thousand Oaks, California 91320

SAGE Publications India Pvt Ltd
B 1/I 1 Mohan Cooperative Industrial Area
Mathura Road
New Delhi 110 044

SAGE Publications Asia-Pacific Pte Ltd
3 Church Street
#10-04 Samsung Hub
Singapore 049483

First published 2022

Editor: Amy Thornton
Senior project editor: Chris Marke
Project management: River Editorial
Marketing manager: Lorna Patkai
Cover design: Wendy Scott
Typeset by: C&M Digitals (P) Ltd, Chennai, India
Printed in the UK

Library of Congress Control Number: 2021942051

British Library Cataloguing in Publication Data

A catalogue record for this book is available from the British Library

ISBN 978-1-5297-5483-4
ISBN 978-1-5297-5482-7 (pbk)

At SAGE we take sustainability seriously. Most of our products are printed in the UK using FSC papers and boards. When we print overseas we ensure sustainable papers are used as measured by the PREPS grading system. We undertake an annual audit to monitor our sustainability.

CONTENTS

ABOUT THE AUTHORS

Mark Patmore is a former senior lecturer in mathematical education in the School of Education at Nottingham Trent University and until recently an associate lecturer at the University of Derby. He has also worked in teacher education with Bishop Grosseteste University and with training providers in supplying subject knowledge courses for intending teachers of mathematics. Mark has been involved with assessing and verifying a range of educational qualifications. He is the author or co-author of a number of publications for both GCSE and Key Stage 3 Mathematics.

Sarah Woodhouse is a former senior lecturer in mathematics education in the School of Education at Nottingham Trent University. Prior to this, she provided mathematics, statistics and numeracy support for students following a range of undergraduate courses at the university. She currently works as a freelance writer of mathematics assessments and resources.

Rebecca Petronzi is the English subject leader for Primary Initial Teacher Education programmes at the University of Derby. She is responsible for supporting students to develop their English subject knowledge and pedagogical knowledge in preparation for their teaching and professional careers. She has a passion for children's literature and is the author of a series of research-informed children's books. Rebecca also works on the admissions and outreach team at the University of Derby, supporting and assessing trainees' English skills and capabilities, alongside offering mentoring and support for their functional English development.

Charlotte Mosey is the leader for the BEd and MEdu courses for teacher education programmes at the University of Derby. She teaches a wide range of areas within the programme and specialises in the English and Humanities subjects. Charlotte is passionate about everything pertaining to education. Her philosophy is deep rooted after gaining over 16 years of experience as a Primary School teacher where she led English as a curriculum area. She is an enthusiastic advocate of new initiatives and approaches, many of which she tests on her six-year-old twin daughters.

INTRODUCTION

Initial Teacher Training (ITT) providers are expected to make an assessment of the English and mathematics knowledge of a trainee before Qualified Teacher Status or Early Years Teacher Status is awarded. ITT providers must, as an accreditation requirement, assure that trainees have these skills either during the selection process, or later during the training programme. Any work to address shortfalls in English and mathematics must be undertaken by the trainee teacher in addition to other aspects of their training. It is the trainee's responsibility to secure these fundamental skills, *whereas responsibility for assurance lies with the ITT provider.*

(DfE, 2019a)

This book supports ITT providers and trainees with a resource that allows trainees to:

- audit their own skills

- identify any areas for their development

and provides a structure within which trainees will be able to:

- track progress in their development

- record competence.

The text outlines the 'basic' English and mathematics skills needed by all teachers. It does not include any pedagogy, but covers the essential knowledge, contextualised where possible, that all teachers should have in these two subject areas. It includes audits, examples and practice questions, allowing the reader to identify gaps in their knowledge and understanding and to demonstrate that these have been addressed.

THE ENGLISH SECTION

This section is divided into a general audit, Chapter 1, which is followed by five English topics and a glossary. The chapters are:

Chapter 2: Spoken language and communication skills

Chapter 3: Spelling and vocabulary

Chapter 4: Punctuation

Chapter 5: Grammar

Chapter 6: Comprehension strategies and approaches

Chapter 7: Answers

Chapter 8: Glossary

The chapters provide a variety of contextual examples, be this in the classroom or engaging with professional documentation. *Chapter 2* provides support for spoken language and communication. *Chapters 3 to 5* cover the English subject knowledge specified by the DfE as essential and correlate to a glossary of terminology. *Chapter 6* reflects on professional comprehension skills, which will require engagement with DfE and Ofsted publications to apply a variety of deduction, inference and sequencing skills. Each chapter follows a similar structure, providing examples and explanations to support the completion of the consolidation tasks. Where the tasks have definite answers, these will be provided in the answers chapter at the end of the English section.

THE MATHEMATICS SECTION

Beginning with a brief introduction the content of the mathematics section is as follows:

Chapter 10: Initial audit

Chapter 11: Numbers and calculation

Chapter 12: Calculating with whole numbers

Chapter 13: Fractions, decimals, percentages (including ratio and proportion)

Chapter 14: Estimation and rounding

Chapter 15: Representing and interpreting data

Chapter 16: Problem solving

Chapter 17: Answers

Chapter 18: Glossary

Chapter 19: Further resources

Chapters 12 to 16 contain:

- text with explanations and examples

- some practice questions with fully worked solutions and key points.

PART 1
ENGLISH

INTRODUCTION TO THE ENGLISH SECTION

You will need to consider whether your personal skills in English meet the requirements specified by the DfE.

> Speaking, listening and communicating are fundamental to a teacher's role. Teachers should use standard English grammar, clear pronunciation and vocabulary relevant to the situation to convey instructions, questions, information, concepts and ideas with clarity. Teachers should read fluently and with good understanding.
>
> Writing by teachers will be seen by colleagues, pupils and parents and, as such, it is important that a teacher's writing reflects the high standards of accuracy their professional role demands. They should write clearly, accurately, legibly and coherently using correct spelling and punctuation.

(DfE, 2020a)

The English section starts with a formative and diagnostic audit. The purpose of the audit is to help you identify your strengths and areas for development. This will help you to analyse areas of focus and determine which specific skills you may still need to work on. Each question is referenced to the appropriate chapter that will support you with the contextual knowledge and application of this area. Towards the end of each chapter, there are consolidatory tasks that link to the content covered. This will allow you to reflect upon your progress and identify opportunities to continue to develop these skills.

It is important to note that this book aims to support fundamental English skills appropriate for teaching professionals and, as such, there is no formal expectation to 'pass' this section. Instead, see the materials as a way to support your development and as a signpost for ongoing reflection. However, please reflect honestly and consider how much of this section you feel you need to revise in order to meet the ITT Criteria identified above.

These chapters provide a variety of contextual examples, be this in the classroom or engaging with professional documentation. *Chapter 2* provides support for spoken language and communication, which – to some extent – moves beyond

English and begins to explore metacognitive strategies for all Key Stages. This chapter's consolidatory task is more reflective in nature; expecting you to observe practice and identify questioning skills.

Chapters 3 to 5 cover English subject knowledge specified by the DfE as essential and correlates to a glossary of terminology. *Chapter 6* reflects on professional comprehension skills, which will require you to engage with DfE and Ofsted publications to apply a variety of deduction, inference and sequencing skills. Each chapter follows a similar structure, providing you with examples and explanations to support you in completing the consolidatory tasks. Where the tasks have definite answers, these will be provided in the answers chapter at the end of the English section.

1

INITIAL AUDIT

1. [Refer to chapter 6]

Imagine that you have just read a story. Now connect each of the questions, in column 1, to the correct skill, in column 2.

Question	Skill
Where was the story set?	Understanding
What similarities do you have to the character?	Recalling
Can you describe the main event?	Analysis
If you were ..., how would you have acted?	Applying
How could this text be improved?	Evaluating
Why has the author chosen the word ... ?	Creating

2. [Refer to chapter 2]

Which of the following types of talk are examples of **Presentational talk** and which are examples of **Exploratory talk**?

Justify   Retell   Explain   Instruct   Predict   Report   Compare   Present

Presentational talk	Exploratory talk

3. [Refer to chapter 3]

In each of the following identify the word which is spelt correctly.

(a) Separate   Seperate   Separete

(b) Ocurrance   Occurrence   Occurrance

(c) Difiantly   Definitely   Definitaly

(d) Conscientiously   Conscioustiously   Contientiously

(e) Embarrassment   embarressment   Embarasment

4. [Refer to chapter 4]

Punctuate this sentence with a comma to change the meaning.

I find satisfaction in eating my pupils and my colleagues.

5. [Refer to chapter 4]

Which sentence demonstrates the correct use of an apostrophe for possession?

(a) Charles's application to the lesson was disappointing.

(b) Charles' application to the lesson was disappointing.

6. [Refer to chapter 4]

Identify the mistake.

Its a wonderful opportunity for the staff and pupils alike.

7. [Refer to chapter 4]

Add the correct punctuation to this sentence.

Can we all focus demanded Mr Ferguson I'm waiting for quiet

8. [Refer to chapter 4]

Add a comma into this sentence:

As I left school that evening I checked that I had organised the resources for the following day.

9. [Refer to chapter 5]

Identify the error in the following sentence.

In the headteacher's opinion, the school might not of been put into Special Measures if the stable staffing the school had benefited from earlier had been maintained.

10. [Refer to chapter 5]

Correct the following sentence:

These fabrics is perfect for my curtains.

11. [Refer to chapter 6]

The following extracts are all from the DfE (2014) SEND Code of practice: 0 to 25 years.

Read this extract:

> *Local authorities must ensure that children, young people and parents are provided with the information, advice and support necessary to enable them to participate in discussions and decisions about their support. This should include information on their rights and entitlements in accessible formats and time to prepare for discussions and meetings. From Year 9 onwards, particularly for those with Education, Health and Care plans, local authorities, schools, colleges and other agencies will be involved in the planning for their transition to adult life, the future and how to prepare for it, including their health, where they will live, their relationships, control of their finances, how they will participate in the community and achieve greater independence.*

Which of the following statements summarises this extract?

(a) Local authorities should support children and families to be involved in the decision-making process for their support, including transition into adult living.

(b) Local authorities must decide what support children will have and then communicate this with parents and children, including determining what will happen to young adults transitioning into adult life.

12. [Refers to chapter 6]

For this extract, who is the audience?

(a)   Parents   (b)   Local authorities/schools   (c)   Children

13. [Refer to chapter 6]

For this extract, which of the following would be a suitable heading?

(a) Working together to plan support.

(b) Local authorities to decide on support schools give.

(c) SEND children to continue in school for longer.

14. [Refer to chapter 6]

These summary statements are based on the extract. Put them into the correct order.

(a) Year 9 children with Education, Health and Care plans should be supported in planning their transition to adult life.

(b) Accessible information should be shared on their rights and entitlements.

(c) Families and children must work with local authorities, to determine appropriate support.

15. [Refer to chapter 6]

Is the following statement true or false?

Considering where children with Education, Health and Care plans will live is an important part of transition plans.

2

SPOKEN LANGUAGE AND COMMUNICATION SKILLS

Speaking, listening and communicating are fundamental to a teacher's role. Teachers should use standard English grammar, clear pronunciation and vocabulary relevant to the situation to convey instructions, questions, information, concepts and ideas with clarity. Teachers should read fluently and with good understanding.

(DfE, 2020a)

This chapter will explore the concept of spoken language and communication, explaining and justifying its significance for teachers. There are numerous communication demands placed upon a teacher, from communicating professionally in staff meetings, conveying sometimes difficult messages to parents and the most basic, yet most important, interactions with students. Good teachers not only communicate instructions but also demonstrate a genuine commitment and care for their students, using a skilful blend of tone of voice and body language in order to support and reassure. It is important to note that communication is not just expressive; teachers should be skilled at listening to their students as well as giving clear directions.

THE NATIONAL CURRICULUM AND THE TEACHERS' STANDARDS

The National Curriculum (DfE, 2013, Key Stages 1 & 2) states that students should *'use discussion in order to learn; they should be able to elaborate and explain clearly their understanding and ideas'*. In Key Stage 3, the National Curriculum (DfE, 2013: 2) acknowledges *'the importance of spoken language in students' development across the whole curriculum – cognitively, socially and linguistically'*. It is important for teachers to understand the transition from primary to secondary education by developing their knowledge of what is required for each Key Stage. Furthermore, the Teachers' Standards (DfE, 2011: 11) identifies that teachers must *'demonstrate an understanding of and take responsibility for promoting high standards of literacy,* *articulacy and the correct use of standard English, **whatever the teacher's specialist subject'*** (notice the phrase in bold font).

As a teacher it will be your responsibility to provide opportunities for developing speaking and listening skills both within the taught curriculum and throughout the hidden curriculum (hidden curriculum being those skills taught beyond the National Curriculum related to culture, society, and relationships). Note also that a significant value is placed on teachers modelling key communication strategies including acknowledging and appropriately responding to others in a variety of settings. Indeed, the Initial Teacher Training Core Content Framework (2019a: 15, Standard 3) states that teachers should develop pupils' literacy by *'Modelling and requiring high-quality oral language, recognising that spoken language underpins the development of reading and writing (e.g. requiring pupils to respond to questions in full sentences, making use of relevant technical vocabulary)'.*

TYPES OF TALK

Talk can be applied in a variety of ways including social, communicative, cultural and cognitive approaches. As a result, teachers must provide opportunities to apply different purposes of talk to all educational and social settings. Teachers must prioritise the provision of opportunities for students to be exposed to many different situations to practise their talk, for example answering an open-ended question, debating or reasoning. Pedagogies employed in many lessons across the Key Stages, such as summarising or explaining, are all used regularly to assess understanding and promote individual higher-level thinking.

This table lists some different purposes of talk that can be employed in the classroom:

Presentational talk	Exploratory talk
To give an instruction	To compare
To retell	To justify
To explain (to others)	To explain (to oneself)
To give an opinion	To describe
To report	To speculate/hypothesise/predict
To present	To deduce

THE 'PERFORMER'

It is important to note that teachers 'perform' in a classroom, and in this context their communication strategies and skills will be presented differently compared with operating in a social context; teachers should model speaking and listening skills in different contexts. Language is a social construct and, therefore, for teachers and students, the environment will change styles of communication. The Teachers' Standards (DfE, 2011) identifies that trainees must *'demonstrate an understanding of and take responsibility for promoting high standards of literacy, articulacy and the correct use of standard English, whatever the teacher's specialist subject'*. It is worth noting the effect of accent and dialogue on communication. Accents have emerged over time from variations in the pronunciation of phonemes (letter sounds) within the English alphabet. In a sense, accent is not different to standard English as long as the speaker is using accurate grammar and vocabulary. Dialect is where language, grammar and vocabulary change based on the geographical location. For example, the phrase 'I am going to the shop' is standard English. In a regional dialect, this could be 'Am guin t't shop'. Such variations can also affect vocabulary that is specific to a regional location. For example, what is a rounded sandwich called? Is it a cob? Or is it a roll? It is important to acknowledge the cultural connections in language and that dialects connect people to their social ecosystems. Students should be supported in identifying appropriate situations for standard English, for their regional dialect and in understanding the rich nature of their language development.

Another consideration of the teacher as a 'performer' is modelling effective communication registers. This may include appropriate intonation to engage an audience or convey purpose/meaning but may also represent tone for effect, including emphasis.

COGNITIVE COMMUNICATION AND LANGUAGE OF LEARNING

Alongside opportunities for exploratory talk and social talk, cognitive talk and vocabulary should be explicitly modelled by teachers in all Key Stages. Metacognitive language involves identifying and articulating the cognitive processes undertaken to achieve a task, including planning and evaluating performance. Teachers may support students in this process through questioning. Below is an example of a metacognitive conversation between a teacher and a child.

Year 5 students have been engaged in a guided reading task on a new text about refugees. The teacher is supporting the students to apply previous strategies when accessing new vocabulary within a shared text.

Mr Pear: Can you identify any new words through skim reading the text? What strategies will you use to understand these new words?

Child A: Last week I used a dictionary.

Mr Pear: How did the dictionary help you to understand new words?

Child A: It gave me the meaning.

Mr Pear: Yes, it gave you a definition. What did you do with the definition?

Child B: I tried to think of other words I know that have a similar meaning, then substituted these in the text.

Mr Pear: Why did you do that?

Child B: Because I already know lots of words, so when I find new ones, I can group these words if they mean similar things.

Mr Pear: How did you feel about using that strategy? Did it make the task easier? Did it help you understand the text?

Child B: Yes, but it was very slow. I had to re-read the texts lots of times.

Mr Pear: Hmmm ... so how can we be quicker?

Child C: Sometimes, I use other clues in the text to see if I can understand the meaning. The context sometimes helps me.

Child A: I like that idea! I might try that first, then use a dictionary if I get really stuck.

Mr Pear: Good thinking. Let's try that and monitor how we find it as we work our way through the text.

This conversation is an observation from an upper Key Stage 2 class. Notice that the majority of the teacher's input are questions intended to support learning. Questioning skills could be applied to any classroom situation and any subject.

QUESTIONING

Teachers will use key questioning to support learning and cognitive communication. They will also engage in collaborative conversation to support well-structured explanations and descriptions. Skilful questioning is at the core of effective pedagogies across the curriculum. Closed questions are those that require a one-word answer or short answer and may not allow students to explain and elaborate ideas fully. These, therefore, have low cognitive involvement. In contrast, open-ended questions can enhance learning and challenge thinking, supporting students to ask questions themselves. Questioning is also an effective assessment strategy for responding to and developing students' learning in a way which addresses Teacher Standards 2, 5 and 6.

The following table lists some of the key phrases that may be used when questioning. The table is created considering some aspects of Bloom's Taxonomy.

Closed/convergent questions	Open/divergent questions			
Recall Retell Remembering	Understand	Apply	Evaluate/ Analyse	Create
• Can you list...? • How many...? • Did you see...?	• Describe how... • Explain how... • Tell me about...	• Think about how... • Can you choose which...why? • How will you plan...?	• Think about why... • Justify why... • Can you evaluate why...?	• How will this help you to design/ plan...?

Source: Adapted from Bloom et al. (1956).

This chapter has discussed the importance of spoken language and communication and its significance for teachers. Teachers communicate when supporting students with their own development when building relationships and effective classroom management. Our ability to communicate is something we often take for granted and we do not evaluate the strategies that we use in day-to-day life or consider the impact our style of communication and choice of language has on students and others. We have identified the need to model these skills both explicitly and implicitly to students. Furthermore, we have considered the use of questioning to develop students' thinking and communication skills.

CONSOLIDATION TASK

The nature of this book is to provide support in developing the fundamental skills for a professional career. Communication is a key element of this journey regardless of Key Stage, but by its very nature can be a challenge to assess and analyse personally. As such, the task provided for this chapter requires self-evaluation.

Consider observing communication exchanges between adults and students and students with their peers. You may be able to find examples online if you do not have access to placement/volunteer work.

See how many questions are asked during these exchanges and what types of questions these may be. The table above will help to support you with this task.

3

SPELLING AND VOCABULARY

Writing by teachers will be seen by colleagues, pupils and parents and, as such, it is important that a teacher's writing reflects the high standards of accuracy their professional role demands. They should write clearly, accurately, legibly and coherently using correct spelling and punctuation.

(DfE, 2020a)

As the criteria state, teachers' writing will be seen; for example, on whiteboards, in books, in letters and on displays. Teachers will be seen as ambassadors for accurate spelling, punctuation and grammar.

We live in a world with spell check and predictive text. Most important communications are written digitally and therefore automatically checked by a computer programme, although they adopt American spelling principles which can be different from UK conventions. For example: *color* and *colour*; in measurement: *meter* and *metre*, *liter* and *litre*. So it is still important to know how to spell, and to check spellings in a dictionary if you are unsure.

This chapter gives you some ways in which to approach spelling. But you may decide that the best approach, given the complexities of the English language, is to learn the words that you have difficulty with.

DOUBLE CONSONANTS

[Note. Vowel and consonant: there are five vowels in English: *A, E, I, O, U*. All the other letters are consonants. Note, the letter y, although classed as a consonant and used as one in words such as *yellow* or *young*, is often used as a vowel with an -i sound in words such as *fly* or *cry*.]

A common problem for adults is knowing when to use a double consonant:

accommodate	*apprentice*	*committee*	*disappoint*
innumerable	*misspell*	*professional*	

Unfortunately, there is no easy way to remember words like these. It does help if you notice those words that you know give you trouble. Look at the following list of some double-consonant words and copy out any that you suspect have been problematic for you in the past. When you have a list, look at each word in turn, remember the whole word, its sequences of letters, its prefix and suffix (if any), and try to write it again. Then check it.

abbreviate	acclimatise	address
allowed	apparent	appear
apprentice	approach	appropriate
approve	approximate	assess
challenge	commensurate	commit/committed
correspondence	correspondent	curriculum
disappear	dissipate	embarrass
exaggerate	excellent	grammar
grip/gripped	happily	harass
immeasurable	(in)efficient	millennium
miscellaneous	miscellany	necessary
occur/occurred	occurrence	omit/omission
opportunity	parallel	passage
permissible	permission	possess
proceed (but precede)	questionnaire	recommend
recur/recurrence	satellite	succeed
success	succinct	terrible
till (but until)	truthfully	vacillate

Some words like *fulfil* end in a single consonant. This is doubled if either -ed or -ng is added. For example:

fulfil becomes *fulfilling*

commit becomes *committing*

begin becomes *beginning*.

HOMOPHONES, HETERONYMS AND HOMONYMS

One of the main reasons for spelling words the way we do is that the spellings represent the sounds spoken. But spellings have evolved over a long period and this is not always the case.

Homophones are words that sound alike but are written or spelt differently and they do not mean the same thing. Common homophones include:

aloud/allowed	*hare/hair*	*wear/where*	*ate/eight*
pear/pair/pare	*lead/led*	*sore/saw*	*doe/dough*
lent/leant	*practice/practise*	*read/red*	*weight/wait*
their/they're/there	*whether/weather*	*meet/meat*	*due/dew*

Heteronyms are words which are spelt the same but have different meanings and different pronunciations, and these may lead to confusion when spelling.

Common heteronyms include:

Close – e.g. *close the door*   and   *I feel close to him.*

Desert – e.g. *you cannot desert your post*   and   *the desert can get very hot and dry.*

Homonyms are words which are spelt and pronounced the same but have different meanings.

Common homonyms include:

Lie – e.g. *I am going for a lie down*   and   *he cannot lie about his age.*

Book – e.g. *I am going to read this book*   and   *I will book a table at your favourite restaurant.*

There are some problems associated with spelling as a word sounds: One common error arises from the words *'could have'*. *'Could have'* is often abbreviated to *'could've'* and the pronunciation of *'could've'* is almost identical to that of *'could of'* so phrases like *'she could of caught the bus'* will often be seen although they are incorrect. (Similar issues arise with *'should've'*, *'must've'*, *'would've'*.)

There are also problems with the different spelling of nouns and verbs:

Practice is a noun, e.g. *doctor's practice. Practise is a verb*, e.g. *I will practise the guitar.*

Effect is a noun, e.g. *the butterfly effect.* Affect is a verb, e.g. *how will this affect the budget?*

Advice is a noun, e.g. *take my advice. Advise is a verb*, e.g. *I'd advise you not to give advice.*

Hint: If you could say *'the'* before a word, it is a noun and will end in -ice. If you could say *'I'* or *'you'* or *'we'* or *'they'* before a word, it is a verb and will end in -ise.

MORPHOLOGY

Morphology is the study of how words are formed and their relationship to other words in the same language. Thinking about morphology may help with spelling.

You might consider associated root words to help with spelling. A root word is a basic word with no prefix or suffix added to it. (A prefix is a string of letters that go at the start of a word; a suffix is a string of letters that go at the end of a word.) By adding prefixes and suffixes to a root word we can change its meaning. So, for *definitely*, the root word is *finite*. The word *finite* means limited or 'having a boundary'. Taking this one step further, the '*nite*' part of *finite* is very different to the word '*night*', so will have a different spelling. The most common mistake in this word is to spell it as '*defin-a-tely*'. When broken down to the root word, *finite* would not sound right if it was spelt *fin-a-te*. This approach will also provide support when spelling other words with the same root. For instance, spelling *destruction* (root word *struct*), enables the spelling of *restructure, construction* and *obstructed*.

The English language has many suffixes. The following are some common ones:

Suffix	Examples
-ent or -ant	assistant, consultant, student, different, dependent, excellent
-ible or -able	irascible, inhabitable, drinkable, accountable, avoidable
-ing	going, having, taking, running
-ise	stabilise, characterise, symbolise, visualise, specialise
-ate	differentiate, liquidate, pollinate, duplicate, fabricate
-fy	classify, exemplify, simplify, justify
-ly	lovely, readily, fully
-en	awaken, fasten, shorten, moisten
-ful	beautiful, peaceful, careful
-ism	Marxism, Thatcherism, organism
-ment	development, punishment, unemployment
-ion	alteration, demonstration, expansion, inclusion, admission
-er	advertiser, driver, computer, silencer
-age	breakage, wastage, package
-al	denial, proposal, refusal, dismissal
-ence or -ance	preference, dependence, interference, attendance
-ery	bribery, robbery, misery
-ship	friendship, citizenship, leadership
-ity	ability, similarity, responsibility, curiosity

(Continued)

Suffix	Examples
-ness	darkness, preparedness, consciousness
-cy	urgency, efficiency, frequency
-al	central, political, national, optional, professional
-ive	attractive, effective, imaginative, repetitive
-ous	continuous, dangerous, famous
-less	endless, homeless, careless, thoughtless

Many spelling difficulties occur around suffixes. There are some spelling rules, but beware – they do not always apply.

- Change the y to an i before adding a suffix. For example:

  ready becomes *readiness*

  easy becomes *easiest*

  happy becomes *happiness*

  angry becomes *angrily.*

- This does not apply to the suffix -ing. For example:

  supply becomes *supplier, supplied, supplies* but keeps the y to form *supplying*

  reply becomes *replied, replies* but keeps the y to form *replying.*

- Drop the silent e when adding a suffix that starts with a vowel such as -ion or -ing. For example:

  educate becomes education

  debate becomes debating.

  However, if the word ends in -ge or -ce this does not apply. For example:

  change becomes *changeable*

  notice becomes *noticeable.*

  And do not drop the silent e when adding a suffix that starts with a consonant. For example:

  care becomes *careful, careless.*

- When adding -ly if the word ends with l then the l should be doubled. For example:

  hopeful becomes hopefully

  faithful becomes faithfully.

- When adding -ly to words ending in e, -ly is just added. For example:

  love becomes *lovely*

  absolute becomes *absolutely.*

- Keep the y at the end of words when the word ends in a vowel and y. For example:

  joy becomes *joyful, joyous, enjoyable.*

- Double the final consonant when adding -ed or -ing to verbs with a short vowel sound. For example:

  rap becomes *rapping, rapper, rapped.*

  However, when the verb has a long vowel sound, the final consonant does not need doubling. For example:

  leap becomes *leaper, leaped, leaping.*

OTHER SPELLING RULES

Spelling rules should come with red flags because sometimes they do not work. For example, a well-known rule is 'i before e except after c', but it is worth noting that it does not apply when the middle sound is a, as in *neighbour* or *eight*, or when the c makes a sh sound, such as in sufficient.

Here are some of the other rules you may come across:

- Add es when the word ends in s, x, z, ch or sh; for example: *bushes, churches.*
- A word with one syllable and one vowel needs a double consonant before a suffix. For example: *fatter, fattest.*
- If the word ends in a vowel followed by a y (such as the word *day*), simply add an s (to form *days*). If the word has a consonant before the y, remove the y and add -ies. For example: *sky* becomes *skies.*

MNEMONICS AND MEMORY TRICKS

Mnemonics may be useful to help with the spelling of words. For instance, a mnemonic for necessary is '*one collar, two sleeves*'.

Others examples of mnemonics are:

- This word can *accommodate* a double c and a double m
- Never *be**lie**ve* a lie

- *Generally,* a general is your best ally

- Goofy Gregg loves to *exaggerate*

Note: You may decide it is easier to learn the spellings themselves than to learn the rules, exceptions and mnemonics.

VOCABULARY

Part of the professional role of the teacher involves accurately using vocabulary appropriate to the situation. Colloquialisms, jargon and 'slang' should be avoided when writing in this professional context.

Homophones, heteronyms and homonyms have been discussed earlier in this chapter and you need to be aware of the correct word to use in a particular situation.

Some commonly misused examples are:

Abuse/misuse/ disabuse	Abuse	To treat something or someone so badly that it or they are damaged
	Misuse	To use something incorrectly
	Disabuse	To show someone that their thinking is wrong
Acute/chronic (as in illness)	Acute	Sudden and severe but short-lived
	Chronic	Persists for a long time
Aggravate/annoy	Aggravate	Make worse
	Annoy	Irritate
Alternate/alternative	Alternate	Going back and forth between two things
	Alternative	Other
Among/between	Among	Use between for two things and among for more than two. So, 'between class 7A and class 7B' and 'among the students in Y7'
	Between	
Amount/number	Amount	Use this word for things that are measured, not counted, e.g. the amount of rain; the amount of sand
	Number	Use this for things that are counted, e.g. the number of people; the number of grains of sand
Complement/ compliment	Complement	Go together, e.g. the wine complements the fish
	Compliment	Say something nice, e.g. I want to compliment you on your work
Continual/continuous	Continual	Happening over and over again
	Continuous	Happening all the time

Forward/foreword	Forward	To advance, to move forward
	Foreword	A passage of text before the main part of a book
Imply/infer	Imply	Suggesting or hinting at something
	Infer	A listener infers something based on what they hear (something that might have been implied)
Lend/loan	Lend	This is a verb, e.g. I lend money to you
	Loan	This is a noun, e.g. I take out a loan
Less/fewer	Less	Not as much. Use with non-countable nouns, e.g. less traffic than yesterday
	Fewer	Not as many. Use with countable nouns, e.g. fewer cars than yesterday
Loose/lose	Loose	Not tight
	Lose	Be unable to find, or have taken away
Older/elder	Older	In a time sense – he is older than me
	Elder	Used to denote respect, e.g. an elder statesman
Principal/principle	Principal	Main, e.g. the head of a school or college
	Principle	A general rule
Stationary/stationery	Stationary	Not moving
	Stationery	Paper and pens, etc.
Their/there/they're	Their	Belongs to them
	There	Refers to a place or position
	They're	Contraction of 'they are'
Weather/whether	Weather	Rain/sun/storms, etc.
	Whether	The first of two alternatives (followed by 'or')

CONSOLIDATION TASK

Complete each sentence with the correct word taken from options given.

1. When the students received their GCSE results, most were _____ to see they had passed.

   Options: releived, relieved, releeved, releaved

2. Following the purchase of a new scheme, the maths team met to discuss the _____.

   Options: implamnetation, implementation, implimentation, implementasion

(Continued)

3. Her parents were _____ upset when their holiday had to be postponed.

    Options: justifiable, justifiably, justifibly, justifeiably

4. After several anti-social events, the school invested in a high-quality _____ system.

    Options: surveillance, surveillence, surviellance, suviellence

5. The decision was made by the school _____ but not the school council.

    Options: comittee, comitee, commitee, committee

6. They had a vote to ensure the process was _____.

    Options: democratic, dimocratic, demockratic, demicratic

7. The head was disappointed – this behaviour was _____.

    Options: unacceptable, unaceptable, unnacepteable, unnaceptible

8. Teachers need to make sure they plan next steps that are _____ – ensuring progress for all learners.

    Options: acheevable, acheivable, achievable, achieveable

9. The headteacher _____ with the parents.

    Options: liased, liaised, leased, leeased

10. In order to have a positive learning environment, it is _____ for all staff to be responsible for monitoring behaviour.

    Options: neccessary, necesary, necessery, necessary

11. The school offered _____ tickets to people from the care home.

    Options: complimentary, complementary

12. _____ students turned up for football than expected.

    Options: less, fewer

13. Based on what she said, I _____ that my work was not good enough

    Options: implied, inferred

14. They argued _____ for a week.

    Options: continually, continuously

4

PUNCTUATION

Writing by teachers will be seen by colleagues, pupils and parents and, as such, it is important that a teacher's writing reflects the high standards of accuracy their professional role demands. They should write clearly, accurately, legibly and coherently using correct spelling and punctuation.

(DfE, 2020a)

Using punctuation correctly enables you to communicate accurately and your reader to understand easily what is being communicated. Punctuation enables sections of writing to be emphasised; it can alter or clarify the meaning of sentences and create a sense of rhythm. Unlike spelling, there is a personal element to the choice of punctuation. The conventions have evolved over time, and some punctuation (for example, the use of ellipses) is, in part, down to personal preference. One of the most important things to remember when punctuating is to be consistent.

Teachers are expected to be able to read and use punctuation correctly, especially in those texts that they are likely to encounter or to produce as part of their professional work. Knowing what punctuation is required, and where it should be implemented, reveals both an awareness of the reader's needs and, fundamentally, a high degree of literacy.

(Bond *et al.*, 2018: 28)

So what are the main elements of punctuation?

Capital letters are required at the beginning of sentences; for the pronoun 'I'; and for all proper nouns. A proper noun is the name of a particular person, place or thing. For example, Mrs Smith, Colin, America, Nottingham, Saturn and Microsoft are all proper nouns.

Question marks are required to indicate the end of a sentence that is asking a question. For example: *What time is assembly today? Can you join me for the meeting after school?*

Exclamation marks are used (sparingly) for emphasis. They can be used at the end of a sentence or a short phrase which expresses strong feeling, for example, *'I refuse to do that!'* Exclamation marks are also commonly used after interjections (words or phrases that are used to exclaim, command or protest, such as *'Wow!' or 'Oh!' or 'Well done!'*).

Full stops are used at the end of sentences that are not questions or exclamations, to denote that a sentence has finished. They tell the reader to pause.

Commas are used to break up sentences and to indicate to the reader where a short pause is intended. They make long sentences easier to read. Commas are used to mark the break between the main clause and a subordinate clause in a sentence. For example, *The student, who had come into class late, went straight to their seat.* Here, the main clause is *The student went straight to their seat* and the subordinate clause is *who had come to class late.* If in doubt, read the sentence to yourself without the words between the commas. If it makes sense, the commas are probably in the correct place.

Sometimes only one comma is required to break up a complex sentence.

For example:

After break, I went back into the classroom. I revisited the school, but it was not as I remembered it.

Note that in both these examples, it is possible to leave out the commas, and this is common in modern usage:

After break I went back into the classroom. I revisited the school but it was not as I remembered it.

This does subtly change the emphasis of the sentence, but generally would not matter if you are writing for information.

Commas are also used in lists. For example, Tony, Rashid, Su and Alexa presented their work to the class; My favourite holiday destinations are France, Spain and Portugal.

If you write dialogue, a comma ends the text before or after the spoken words begin or end: *Gopal said, 'Come along with me'; 'Come along with me,' said Gopal.* But if the dialogue ends with a question mark or an exclamation mark, there is no need for a comma: *'What a fantastic response!' the teacher said; 'Group A,' he called, 'Would you like to join in?'*

The positioning of commas can completely change the meaning of a sentence. There is an important difference between Let's eat Grandma and Let's eat, Grandma.

Colons follow independent clauses (clauses that could stand alone as sentences) and can be used to present an explanation, draw attention to something, or join ideas together.

For example:

He achieved what he had worked for: he really deserved that excellent grade.

Here, the colon joins what could be two sentences and makes a link between them.

Or:

Every living organism can be classified into one of five kingdoms: animals, plants, fungi, protists and prokaryotes. The colon in this sentence signals that you are about to learn the names of the five kingdoms. It could be replaced by 'which are'. Another example would be, For the next PE lesson, please bring the following: trainers, track-suit, a drink and a snack.

Colons can also be used before a reference or direct speech instead of a comma.

For example:

Gopal said: "Come along with me."

Or perhaps:

The headline read: "Teachers praised for their hard work."

Semicolons create a break between two clauses that is more definitive than a comma but less final than a full stop. They often replace a conjunction such as 'and' or 'but'. The group of words that comes both before and after the semicolon should form a completed sentence. For a semicolon to be appropriate, these two sentences should share a close, logical connection.

For example:

Go to the library to do some research; Monday mornings are pretty quiet there.

Here, the semicolon is replacing a full stop.

Or:

Abi has gone to the library; Tom has gone to play football.

Here it is replacing 'and'.

Increasingly, people use a dash instead of a semicolon, especially in emails, but this is slightly more informal. For example, *Go to the library to do some research – Monday mornings are pretty quiet there.*

Semicolons can also be used within detailed lists of information. For example, The spring assessment results revealed the following: 89% of students were able to fully complete the first comprehension task within the time allocated; over one-quarter of children achieved above expected standard in the test; half demonstrated significant progress in this area.

Brackets/parentheses can be used to provide extra information within a sentence. A benefit of this form of punctuation is that it can be easily seen by the reader: *Harriet (in Year 6) is accomplished at writing rhyming poems.* If you take the bracketed words out, the rest of the words must read as a complete sentence.

Inverted commas (also called 'speech marks') are used to show words that are being spoken as direct speech or that are lifted as a quotation from another written source. Sentence punctuation must be placed inside the inverted commas. For example, *'"I wonder what kind of punctuation we should use here?" asked Mrs Smith'*. Or *'Mr Brown asked, "Who knows how to punctuate confidently?"'*

Speech marks are sometimes shown with double inverted commas ("..."), as in the example above and quotation marks with single ones ('...'): *'John introduced the debate. "The question 'is mathematics invented or discovered?' is the topic for discussion" he said.'* The only rule is: use double quotation marks within single quotation marks and use single quotation marks within double quotation marks, as shown in the last example. Here, single inverted commas have been used to indicate where our example begins and ends; double inverted comments have been used to indicate what John said; and single have been used again (inside the double) to indicate the question to be debated.

Either single or double inverted commas can be used to indicate speech.

Hyphens are used to join two or more words serving as a single adjective before a noun, for example 'an over-arching concern' or 'a well-known author'.

Hyphens in compound words can show that there is a link and an associated significance such as 'check-in' or 'eye-opener'.

Sometimes hyphens are used to avoid an unfortunate conjunction of letters: 're-sign a petition' (as opposed to resign from a job) or 'shell-like' (to avoid three letter Ls together).

Some words are not hyphenated but are closed compounds and are presented as one word, for example 'bookshop' or 'lighthouse'. You may see words presented differently in different sources: punctuation usage changes over time and words that previously were written with hyphens are now presented as one word. Would you write 'playground' or 'play-ground' or even 'play ground'?

Apostrophes are *not* used to create plurals, although this incorrect use of apostrophes is often seen in day-to-day life: potatoe's or tomatoe's at the greeengrocer; MOT's seen at garages; or in street names such as Church View Villa's.

Apostrophes have two main uses: to show possession (to demonstrate that something belongs to someone or is linked in some way) and for omission (to show missing letters within a contraction such as don't).

To indicate *possession*, add an apostrophe plus the letter s. For example, *Last week's attendance figures were disappointing in Year 7*. Or *Hannah's handwriting is much improved*. For words such as plurals that already end in an s, add the apostrophe after the final letter. For example, *The boys' work was well considered and included good use of evidence from the text*. For names that end in an s, just add an apostrophe: *Charles' homework is always completed to a high standard*.

Using apostrophes to indicate an *omission* or contraction introduces informality and should not be done in formal documents. Examples of contractions include:

I am – I'm happy that you did that.

Do not – Don't eat sweets in class.

Cannot – Can't you recall that conversation?

I would – I'd prefer it if we could meet tomorrow.

We would – We'd better leave now.

*It is or it has – It's been snowing all day.

*This last example often causes errors in sentence punctuation. *Its* is posses-sive, meaning something belongs to something. For example, *The classroom had display boards on its walls*; or *The school took much pride in its exam results. It's* with an apostrophe means it is or it has: *It's been a long journey, but it was worth it*; or *It's clear to see that the students enjoyed their geography field-trip last week.*

This chapter has highlighted the most commonly used punctuation marks and also included examples to demonstrate their correct use. Punctuation is deployed for a number of reasons: to clarify meaning, to add expression and even provide tone to the written word. Indeed, punctuation can help prose really come alive. There are, of course, a number of pitfalls, particularly with the use of apostrophes and commas. What makes the application of punctuation problematic is the often personal choice relating to a number of applications and the stylistic evolution. As always, consistency is key – alongside a good grasp of the basic rules.

CONSOLIDATION TASK

Read this lesson observation and add in the missing punctuation:

As an NQT you have created clear expectations for the behaviour expected in your class. The science lesson was purposeful orderly and well resourced. The habitat sorting activity was inspiring and engaged all learners. The children needed to crack the code in order to find the final answer to the problem clues were hidden around the classroom. The habitats that were explored included woodlands ponds gardens and cityscapes. Children responded to your questions with confidence you used good open questions including when you asked Why do you think this It was good to observe you deploying support staff. Now con-sider next steps for encouraging the children to co-operate more in a group dis-cussion situation. How can you develop confidence in speaking and listening

5

GRAMMAR

Speaking, listening and communicating are fundamental to a teacher's role. Teachers should use standard English grammar, clear pronunciation and vocabulary relevant to the situation to convey instructions, questions, information, concepts and ideas with clarity. Teachers should read fluently and with good understanding.

(DfE, 2020a)

The Teaching Standards (DfE, 2011) states that trainees should *'promote high standards of literacy, articulacy and the correct use of standard English'*. This is essential in many professional roles but paramount for teachers, who are active role models for children and young adults. Grammar is about sentence structure. The *'correct use of standard English'* is, in large part, about using correct sentence structure in your writing (in association with correct spelling and punctuation).

SENTENCES

One of the most common errors in adult writing is the failure to use proper sentence structure. A sentence is a group of words, usually containing a noun and a verb, that expresses a thought in the form of a statement, question, instruction or exclamation. When written down, rather than spoken, it starts with a capital letter and ends with a full stop. It is difficult to define a sentence exactly as there are many different forms. A sentence will usually contain at least one noun and one verb with the addition of other types of word such as adjectives, adverbs, pronouns and conjunctions. Complex sentences will also have different clauses separated by commas, colons or semicolons. Creative writers may play with the rules, but writing for information needs to obey the rules and conventions. For example, you must ensure that verb tenses are consistent and that the verbs agree with their subjects.

This is a faulty sentence construction:

Concerned about falling numbers in the city's schools so the Director of Education proposed that two primary schools should be merged into one school and the land of the school that was closed was going to be sold for building affordable homes.

It would be better as:

Concerned about falling numbers in the city's schools, the Director of Education proposed that two primary schools should be merged into one school and the land of the school that was closed be sold for building affordable homes.

It is often better to write one or more short sentences, than one long sentence. For example, the sentence above could be rewritten as:

The Director of Education was concerned about falling numbers in the city's schools. She therefore proposed that two primary schools should be merged into one school, and that the land of the school to be closed be sold for building affordable homes.

If you are not sure whether to use a comma or a full stop, use a full stop and begin a new sentence. There is room for personal preference here (sometimes called someone's 'writing style') but your aim should always be to convey information as clearly as possible.

This is a sentence fragment:

If the purpose of the starter activity is to get the lesson off to a brisk start.

This passage has obviously become separated from a sentence of which it was a part and the writer has put in an unnecessary full stop. The original passage might have looked like this:

If the purpose of the starter activity is to get the lesson off to a brisk start, then it needs to be planned with this in mind.

You should pick up sentence fragment errors like these as you read through what you have written.

Most of us learn how to construct sentences by reading books and newspapers, which are (usually) grammatically correct. If you lack confidence writing, it is a good idea to increase the amount of good quality writing that you read, whether fiction, non-fiction or journalism. As you do so, you will begin to learn the strategies authors use and then be able to reproduce this in your own writing.

TENSE AND TENSE INCONSISTENCY

Tense is the aspect of a verb that deals with time. It is possible to use more than one tense in a sentence. For example:

My father was a doctor, I am a doctor and my daughters are going to be doctors.

The verb *was* is a form of the past tense, the verb *am* is a form of the present tense, and *are going to be* is a form of the future tense.

The following example demonstrates lack of consistency in the use of tenses:

Sarah began reading the novel at half-term and finishes it last week.

Began is past tense and *finishes* is present tense, and also note *last week* implies in the past so there is a lack of consistency.

The sentence should read:

Sarah began reading the novel at half-term and finished it last week.

Began and *finished* are both verbs in the past tense so here there is consistency.

Or the sentence could read:

Sarah began reading the novel at half-term and will finish it next week.

Will finish is future tense, but the sentence is grammatically consistent because it could be written as two sentences, both of which have the tense correct:

Sarah began reading the novel at half-term. She will finish it next week.

Another example of inconsistency in a sentence is:

The staff will have finished their marking by the end of Friday and so met the deadline.

In this sentence the staff have not yet completed their marking, so it is not true to say they have met the deadline.

It should be:

The staff will have finished their marking by the end of Friday and so will meet the deadline.

SUBJECT AND VERB AGREEMENT

The subject of a sentence is the person or thing that is doing something. So, in *The cat sits on the mat*, the subject is the cat, because it is doing the sitting. *Sits* is the verb, which tells you what is being done. *The mat* is the object, because it is the thing that is having the sitting done on it. It is very important to ensure that the verb form agrees with the subject. For example, *The cat sit on the mat* is wrong because cat is singular and the verb form is plural. So, the subject and verb do not agree. *The cats sit on the mat* would be correct because here both the subject and verb form are plural.

The common errors here are likely to arise with:

- two nouns (e.g. *French and German*) with a singular verb (e.g. *is*)

- a plural determiner (e.g. *these*) with a singular verb (e.g. *was*)

- a singular determiner (e.g. *this*) with a plural verb (e.g. *were*)

- a singular verb (e.g. *is*) with a non-English plural (e.g. *criteria*)

Example:

A first year undergraduate should receive good support from tutors and from the student union. Nevertheless, they have substantial responsibility.

The noun *undergraduate* is singular but the pronoun, *they*, is plural.

The passage should read, changing the noun into a plural form:

First year undergraduates should receive good support from tutors and from the student union. Nevertheless, they have substantial responsibility.

Or, changing the pronoun into a singular form:

A first year undergraduate should receive good support from tutors and from the student union. Nevertheless, he or she has substantial responsibility.

Some other examples of lack of agreement are:

Some teachers who had been trained in mastery has seen improved results.

Some is plural – it signifies more than one teacher, so it precedes the plural noun *teachers*. It therefore needs the plural verb *have*:

Some teachers who had been trained in mastery have seen improved results.

Sentences can have two singular nouns and a plural verb: *Tom and Helen are going to Spain.* You need to be careful though: both of the following examples are grammatically correct:

Trial and improvement comes naturally to students.

Reading and writing come naturally to students.

This is because trial and improvement is a single problem-solving technique (so needs a singular verb form) whereas reading and writing are two separate things (so need a plural verb form).

An example of a singular determiner with a plural verb is:

Many people taught in the 1960s have a very narrow view of numeracy without realising that that view were limiting.

The second use of 'that' is a singular determiner so it needs a singular verb, *was* instead of *were*, and the sentence should read:

Many people taught in the 1960s have a very narrow view of numeracy without realising that that view was limiting.

You also need to be aware of unusual plurals. For example, *criterion*, which is singular and criteria which is plural. So a sentence like this might be seen:

The research criteria was in dispute.

Was is a singular verb and *criteria* is a plural noun so the sentence ought to read:

The research criteria were in dispute.

PRONOUNS

Pronouns are words that stand in for nouns. Examples are *me, I, he, she, it, them, who.*

People often use *me* and *I* incorrectly when referring to something they did with another person. To solve this issue, consider whether you would refer to 'I' without the other person being present.

For example:

My friend and I are going shopping.

Without your friend, it would still be:

I am going shopping.

In other examples, where you would refer to *me*, if you introduce a second subject, you should still refer to me: *The student gave his homework to me* and *The student gave his homework to Jane and me.*

For the same reason you would write:

The head showed John and me round the school

and not

The head showed John and I round the school.

The relative pronouns are: *who, whom, which, that.* They appear in sentences like these:

The headteacher believed that the school needed a teacher who could develop the new 6th form. After a lot of discussion, the interviewing panel agreed to appoint the candidate whom the headteacher preferred.

It is also possible to leave out the relative pronoun in many cases. This sentence:

She was the one whom they wanted

could also be written as:

She was the one that they wanted.

or

She was the one they wanted

The common error is to use a relative pronoun that is not appropriate. *Which* is the pronoun we use when we are dealing with inanimate things. For example:

The class had read texts which really extended their range of interests and abilities.

It is not appropriate when dealing with people. For example, this sentence is incorrect:

They had chosen the teacher which the headteacher wanted.

It ought to read:

They had chosen the teacher whom the headteacher wanted.

Or:

They had chosen the teacher the headteacher wanted.

When do you use *who* and when do you use *whom*? Whether you should use *who* or *whom* is the same question as whether to use *he* or *him, she* or *her, I* or *me, we* or *us.* It is about whether the person to whom the pronoun refers is the subject or the object of the sentence. Suppose you try the two options in this sentence:

The panel chose the candidate who/whom was best.

Ask yourself whether you would be more likely to write: *She was best,* or: *Her was best.* Clearly you would say *She was best.* That means you would choose *who.* If you wanted to write this sentence: *The headteacher asked the rest of the panel who/whom they liked,* would it make more sense to write: *They liked she* or: *They liked her?* You would choose her and so you would also choose *whom. Whom* is now considered quite formal, and you will often see *who* used (or the pronoun is omitted altogether) when *whom* is grammatically more correct. Consider these alternative sentences:

She opened the letter, even though she was not the person to whom it was addressed.

She opened the letter, even though she was not the person it was addressed to.

The first is grammatically correct, the second is not. But the second is in common usage, would be understood and avoids the use of *whom.* Which sounds better to you? Language evolves, but it is useful to know the rules so that you can make informed choices.

CONSOLIDATION TASK

TENSE

Select the correct option to complete the sentence.

1. I don't consider myself a very gifted person, although I did well enough, but my headteacher father believes I'll make a good teacher and that, although I have always been a little naïve,

   a. life was good.

   b. life being good.

   c. life is good.

   d. life will be good.

2. Whatever I do, my mind fills with thoughts of what could happen if I chose a course where I can't fit in, the other students don't respond, the staff are cold and unhelpful and my tutor

    a. is bad-tempered.

    b. was bad-tempered.

    c. has been bad-tempered.

    d. being bad-tempered.

3. Perhaps the best action for me to take is to talk with friends, at least once I have examined what different areas offer, compared facilities, accommodation and opportunities and

    a. growing a little more sure of myself.

    b. grow a little more sure of myself.

    c. grew a little more sure of myself.

    d. grown a little more sure of myself.

SUBJECT AND VERB AGREEMENT

4. Select the correct word to insert in the box.

    The trouble with both the way I talk and the way I write ☐ that for much of the time I cannot trust myself to remember where I started.

    a. are

    b. were

    c. was

    d. is

5. Select the correct phrase to complete this sentence.

    A friend told me that the likeliest cause of this problem is that the attitude shown towards me by my first English teacher

    a. is quite traumatic for me.

    b. were quite traumatic for me.

    c. was quite traumatic for me.

    d. being quite traumatic for me.

(Continued)

6. Select the phrase that correctly completes the sentence.

As I look ahead, I know that the future, whether I am lucky or not, whether I leave teaching or I stay with it, and whatever anyone else does or says,

    a. was mine to make.

    b. has been mine to make.

    c. will be mine to make.

    d. will have been mine to make.

6

COMPREHENSION STRATEGIES AND APPROACHES

Teachers should read fluently and with good understanding.

(DfE, 2020a)

Students use and apply comprehension skills to support their understanding through all Key Stages and in all subjects. Reading for pleasure, research and initiatives have been a priority in education in recent years, and students must be supported to develop their reading comprehension skills and to acquire not only a love for literature, but also the ability to read for information.

The National Curriculum (DfE, 2013: 4) states that comprehension skills must be developed [in students] through *'high-quality discussion with the teacher'* and from reading a *'range of stories, poems and non-fiction'*. Reading for information and discussing written material is therefore important in all classrooms, not just in English lessons, and all teachers should have these skills themselves so that they can develop them in their students.

English programmes of study: Key Stage 3 The National Curriculum (DfE, 2013: 4) states:

> *students should be taught to: understand increasingly challenging texts through: learning new vocabulary, relating it explicitly to known vocabulary and understanding it with the help of context and dictionaries, making inferences and referring to evidence in the text, knowing the purpose, audience for and context of the writing and drawing on this knowledge to support comprehension, checking their understanding to make sure that what they have read makes sense.*

Previously, trainee teachers were required to pass the skills test for English. Within this, comprehension was a key area, and the test was used to demonstrate a trainee's ability to:

1. identify main points in a text

2. distinguish between facts and opinions

3. retrieve facts and key points

4. make inferences and deductions

5. evaluate meaning and status.

So, the skillset expected of teachers parallels the skillset students acquire throughout different stages and subjects as directed by the National Curriculum.

Summarising a text is a good exercise to test and develop your understanding of it. Summarising requires you to organise, order and paraphrase, so requires a high degree of comprehension. You may be required to summarise when sharing policy documents and other written information with other staff or when providing information to students.

Within this section, the following Ofsted extract will be used to provide examples.

On 17 March 2020, all routine inspections were suspended due to the COVID-19 (coronavirus) pandemic. Since then, teachers, headteachers and support staff have been stepping up to support pupils, families and the communities they serve. We know that this work continues.

We carried out interim visits to schools in autumn 2020. These enabled us to work with school leaders to fully understand the impact of COVID-19 and report on this as part of our national research programme. School leaders told us that they found these visits supportive, saying that the discussion with Her Majesty's Inspectors (HMI) helped them to reflect on their priorities during this difficult time.

Building on this work, from January 2021, we will carry out additional monitoring inspections of schools judged as requires improvement or inadequate. These are not part of our normal programme of monitoring in these schools. They are additional inspections to ensure that leaders and managers are taking effective action to provide education in the current circumstances.

Initially, the majority of these visits will be carried out remotely in response to the latest government guidance and current COVID-19 restrictions. As soon as COVID-19 conditions allow, we will return to all inspections taking place on site. We will continue to carry out on-site visits, or to move remote visits to on-site visits, where inspectors have specific or significant concerns, such as safeguarding or a breakdown in leadership and management.

(OFSTED, 2021)

IDENTIFYING KEY POINTS AND FACTS

In order to identify key points, it may be important to categorise statements. Some of the statements from the Ofsted extract can be categorised as follows:

About Ofsted	About schools	About COVID-19 response
They carried out interim visits to schools in autumn 2020.	They found these visits supportive.	Due to this, remote visits will be carried out.
They will carry out additional monitoring.	They have supported pupils, families and communities.	This resulted in inspections being suspended.

Four key points might be:

1st point	COVID-19 resulted in inspections being temporarily suspended.
2nd point	Schools and staff have worked hard to continue to support their communities and pupils.
3rd point	National research with schools supported Ofsted to understand the impact of COVID-19 on schooling.
4th point	Additional inspections will be carried out to monitor schools that are judged as 'requires improvement'.

Similarly for the same extract, a summary of three key points might be:

Ofsted have conducted interim inspections allowing them to understand the impact of COVID-19 on schooling.

During national lockdown, Ofsted will continue to monitor schools that are requiring improvement. This is in addition to standard inspections.

Ofsted will conduct visits remotely until government advice says it is safe to complete on-site visits.

Key points may be organised under appropriate headings and subheadings. A heading should present a broad view of everything within the piece, whereas subheadings should allow the reader to clearly identify the purpose of sections within the piece.

A potential heading for the Ofsted extract could be:

Ofsted to conduct additional visits in response to COVID-19

Subheadings should identify the content of each section. For example, paragraph 2 of the extract above could have the following subheadings:

National research

School leaders reflect on priorities

Understanding the impact of COVID-19

STATUS OF TEXT

Full comprehension requires deduction and inference. To deduce is to draw a logical conclusion from the information given in the text. To infer is to go beyond the information given in the text, based on your personal experience and knowledge. To read critically and to understand the status of a text, you will need to identify whether a point is being stated with direct evidence, stated with no evidence, implied based on indirect evidence, implied with no evidence, or even contradicted in another part of the text. This will help you to differentiate between facts and opinions and to identify flaws in an argument.

PURPOSE OF THE TEXT

Audience and purpose are other aspects of comprehension. To understand who a text is aimed at, you need to: consider the key messages; infer from the language the level and the type of audience; deduce from relevant information the suitability for the audience. Determining purpose may also require an understanding of the context for the text and knowledge of specific acronyms and terminology. For example, this Ofsted extract talks about schools but is not aimed at children as the language is far too advanced and complex. It could be deduced that the language is aimed at school leaders because of the phrase *leadership and management* and the words *monitoring, effective and improvement*.

The extracts that have been used in this chapter demonstrate the expectations of teachers. You will be expected to read, understand, disseminate and enact key points of different policies and documents. Sometimes, this may require you to clarify key points of policies and rewrite for different stakeholders. For example, policies that influence teaching practice may need to be paraphrased for parents to engage with. Another focus for teachers is to engage with research-informed practice. You may therefore need to apply your comprehension skills to academic reading.

CONSOLIDATION TASK

Use the following two extracts to answer the questions below.

What does the Newly Qualified Teacher Survey (2017) tell us about workload? The 2017 NQT survey, completed by 1,639 respondents between 28 August and 9 October 2017, asked a variety of questions, including those specific to workload: Two-thirds (65%) of NQTs who were in progress or had completed their induction year said they had discussed what their workload would be like with their training provider or placement school(s). Among those who had discussed what their workload would be like, the majority said their workload in their induction years was as they expected, though 28% said it was bigger than expected. NQTs were also asked the extent to which they felt encouraged – by either their training provider or their placement school(s) – to reduce unnecessary workload around marking, planning and teaching resources, and data management. Up to half of NQTs (26% to 52%) felt they had been encouraged to at least a fair extent to reduce unnecessary workload across the three areas. NQTs were most likely to report feeling encouraged to at least a fair extent to reduce workload around planning and teaching resources, followed by marking and data management. Across all three areas, NQTs were significantly more likely to feel they had been encouraged to reduce unnecessary workload a fair amount or a great deal by their placement school(s) than by their training provider.

(DfE, 2019b)

[T]oo often, new teachers have not enjoyed the support they need to thrive, nor have they had adequate time to devote to their professional development. The Early Career Framework (ECF) underpins an entitlement to a fully funded, two-year package of structured training and support for early career teachers linked to the best available research evidence. The package of reforms will ensure new teachers have dedicated time set aside to focus on their development. Our vision is for the ECF to build on high-quality Initial Teacher Training (ITT) and become the cornerstone of a successful career in teaching.

(DfE, 2019c)

(Continued)

1. Who is being referred to in the following statements? Tick the correct box.

	NQTs	Teachers that are part of the Early Career Framework	Schools
The survey was completed by 1,639 respondents.			
Staff will receive a fully funded, two-year package.			
This group was encouraged to minimise its workload by schools.			
... are more likely than training providers to encourage NQTs to minimise workload.			

2. Sequence the following statements in the order that they appear in the second extract.

   (a) Teachers will require dedicated time to engage in this framework.

   (b) Teachers new to the profession have had limited opportunity for professional development.

   (c) It is the aim of the ECF to bridge the gap between ITT and teaching careers.

   (d) A new framework has been introduced which supports two years of structured training.

3. Which heading is most suitable for the extracts above?

   Supporting early career teachers with reducing workload and professional development.

   NQTs can't handle the work and are struggling to teach.

   The Early Careers Framework is better than ITT support.

4. Determine which of the following statements are deduction or inference. Tick the correct box.

	Deduction – supported by the text	Inference – implied to be the case	Deduction – this contradicts the text explicitly or there is no evidence for this	Inference – the text implicitly contradicts this
One-third of NQTs said they had discussed what their workload would be like.				
Training providers did not encourage reduction of workload.				
28% of NQTs said their workload was bigger than expected.				
NQTs were less likely to feel they had been encouraged to reduce unnecessary workload.				

7

ANSWERS

CHAPTER 1: INITIAL AUDIT

1. [Refer to Chapter 6]

Question	Correct skill
Where was the story set?	Recalling
What similarities do you have to the character?	Applying
Can you describe the main event?	Understanding
If you were ..., how would you have acted?	Creating
How could this text be improved?	Evaluating
Why has the author chosen the word ...?	Analysis

2. [Refer to Chapter 2]

Presentational talk	Exploratory talk
Retell, Instruct, Report, Present	Justify, Explain, Predict, Compare

3. [Refer to Chapter 3]
   (a) The correct spelling is: separate
   (b) The correct spelling is: occurrence
   (c) The correct spelling is: definitely
   (d) The correct spelling is: conscientiously
   (e) The correct spelling is: embarrassment

4. [Refer to Chapter 4]

   The correct response is: I find satisfaction in eating, my pupils and my colleagues.

5. [Refer to Chapter 4]

    (b) is correct: Charles' application to the lesson was disappointing.

6. [Refer to Chapter 4]

    The correct response is: It's a wonderful opportunity for the staff and pupils alike.

7. [Refer to Chapter 4]

    The correct response is: 'Can we all focus?' demanded Mr Ferguson, 'I'm waiting for quiet!'

8. [Refer to Chapter 4]

    The correct response is: As I left school that evening, I checked that I had organised the resources for the following day.

9. [Refer to Chapter 5]

    The sentence should read: '… the school might not have been …'

10. [Refer to Chapter 5]

    The sentence should read either 'These fabrics are perfect for my curtains' or 'This fabric is perfect for my curtains'.

11. [Refer to Chapter 6]

    The correct response is (a):

    Local authorities should support children and families to be involved in the decision-making process for their support, including transition into adult living.

    Statement (a) is **correct** because the first sentence of the extract identifies children, young people and parents as the subjects to whom information is provided – allowing them to make informed decisions.

    Statement (b) is **incorrect** as this implies the local authorities decide on behalf of families and children.

12. [Refer to Chapter 6]

    (b) Local authorities/schools

13. [Refer to Chapter 6]

    (a) Working together to plan support.

14. [Refer to Chapter 6]

    (c) Families and children must work with local authorities, to determine appropriate support.

(b) Accessible information should be shared on their rights and entitlements.

(a) Year 9 children with Education, Health and Care plans should be supported in planning their transition to adult life.

15. [Refer to Chapter 6]

The statement is true.

CONSOLIDATION TASKS

CHAPTER 3: SPELLING AND VOCABULARY

1. relieved

2. implementation

3. justifiably

4. surveillance

5. committee

6. democratic

7. unacceptable

8. achievable

CHAPTER 4: PUNCTUATION

As an NQT you have created clear expectations for the behaviour expected in your class. The science lesson was purposeful, orderly and well-resourced. The habitat sorting activity was inspiring and engaged all learners. The children needed to crack the code in order to find the final answer to the problem (clues were hidden around the classroom). The habitats that were explored included: woodlands, ponds, gardens and cityscapes. Children responded to your questions with confidence; you used good open questions including: 'Why do you think this?' and 'How do you know?' It was good to observe you deploying support staff. Now, consider next steps for encouraging the children to co-operate more in a group discussion situation. How can you develop confidence in speaking and listening?

CHAPTER 5: GRAMMAR

1. Answer (d)   'will be' is future tense as is 'I'll make'.

2. Answer (a)   in the example all the verbs are in the present tense.

3. Answer (d) 'grown' makes most sense because it is the only option that fits the verb form 'have examined'.

4. Answer (d) the subject is 'trouble' which is singular, so the verb must be singular.

5. Answer (b) the subject, 'attitudes', is plural so the verb has to be plural.

6. Answer (c) the tense not only fits the grammar but also the obvious sense of the future.

CHAPTER 6: COMPREHENSION STRATEGIES AND APPROACHES

1.

	NQTs	Teachers that are part of the Early Career Framework	Schools
The survey was completed by 1,639 respondents.	✓		
Staff will receive a fully funded, two-year package.		✓	
This group was encouraged to minimise its workload by schools.	✓		
... are more likely than training providers to encourage NQTs to minimise workload.			✓

2.

[1st] (b) Teachers new to the profession have had limited opportunity for professional development.

[2nd] (d) A new framework has been introduced which supports two years of structured training.

[3rd] (a) Teachers will require dedicated time to engage in this framework.

[4th] (c) It is the aim of the ECF to bridge the gap between ITT and teaching careers.

3.

Supporting early career teachers with reducing workload and professional development.

4.

	Deduction - supported by the text	Inference - implied to be the case	Deduction - this contradicts the text explicitly or there is no evidence for this	Inference - the text implicitly contradicts this
One-third of NQTs said they had discussed what their workload would be like.		X		
Training providers did not encourage reduction of workload.				X
28% of NQTs said their workload was bigger than expected.	X			
NQTs were less likely to feel they had been encouraged to reduce unnecessary workload.			X	

8

GLOSSARY

This is a list of some common terms that you may encounter.

Abbreviation	A shortened word or phrase.
Abstract noun	Denotes an idea, quality or state rather than a concrete object.
Accent	Distinctive way of pronouncing a language.
Active voice	Subject of the sentence performs the action as denoted by the verb.
Adjectives	Words that are used to describe a noun, e.g. *beautiful, enormous*.
Adverbial phrase	Phrase which includes an adverbial to determine how something is done, e.g. *As quickly as she could.*
Antonym	A word which is the opposite of another word, e.g. *hot* and *cold*.
Apostrophe	A punctuation mark used to mark omissions and possessives of nouns and pronouns.
Audience	Observers and listeners.
Brackets (parentheses)	Punctuation marks used to isolate a section of text.
Clause	A part of a sentence.
Colon	This punctuation mark is used to introduce an explanation. The phrase that comes after the colon usually explains or expands on what came before it. It is also used before a list or quotation.
Comma	There are four types of comma: the listing comma, the joining comma, the gapping comma and bracketing commas.
Complex sentence	These require at least one subordinate clause that adds more detail and information to the sentence, e.g. *Elizabeth realised she had forgotten her keys, so she ran quickly back to her house.*

Compound sentence	A sentence that has at least two independent clauses joined by a comma, semicolon or conjunction.
Conjunction	A word used to connect clauses or sentences or to coordinate words in the same clause.
Deduction	Answering questions based on the information given in a text.
Determiner	Words placed in front of a noun to make it clear what the noun refers to.
Dialect	A form of a language which is specific to a region or social group.
Etymology	The study of the origin of words and the way in which their meanings have changed throughout history.
Executive function	A set of mental skills that include working memory, flexible thinking and self-control.
Grapheme	A written symbol that represents a sound (phoneme). This can be a single letter, or could be a sequence of letters, such as ai, sh, igh, tch, etc.
Heteronyms	Words which are spelt the same but have different meanings and different pronunciations.
Homonyms	Words which are spelt and pronounced the same but have different meanings. *I am going for a lie down; he cannot lie about his age.*
Homophone	Words that sound alike but are spelt differently and do not mean the same thing, e.g. *throne, thrown.*
Hyphen	A punctuation mark used to join words and to separate syllables of a single word.
Inference	Making an inference involves reading between the lines using known information from the text.
Metacognition	The processes used to plan, monitor and assess personal understanding and performance.
Morphology	The study of the internal structure of words.
Non-restrictive clause	This provides additional information to a sentence, often a proper noun or a common noun that refers to something unique. Commas are deployed to show that the information is additional.
Phonemes	Distinct units of sound, e.g. *p in pot, d in dog.*
Prefix	A word or letter placed in front of another, e.g. **un**tidy.
Preposition	A word that explains where or when something is in relation to something else, e.g. *under, above.*

Relative clause	A relative clause can be used to give additional information about a noun.
Restrictive clause	A clause that restricts or defines the meaning of a noun or noun phrase and gives important information about the noun in the sentence. It is not separated from the rest of the sentence by the use of commas.
Semicolon	The semicolon can help you join closely connected ideas in a sentence, it can also break up a list that contains longer phrases.
Sequencing	To arrange in a particular order.
Simile	A figure of speech that compares two different things in an interesting way.
Standard English	The form of the English language widely accepted as the correct form.
Suffix	A letter or group of letters that goes on the end of a word.
Synonym	A word or phrase that means exactly or nearly the same as another word or phrase in the same language, e.g. *blistering* is a synonym of *hot*.
Verb	A word used to describe an action.

9

FURTHER RESOURCES AND REFERENCES

RESOURCES

BBC Teach – Skillswise	www.bbc.co.uk/teach/skillswise
BiteSize	www.bbc.com/education
British Council – Learn English	https://learnenglish.britishcouncil.org/skills
Foundation Online Learning	www.foundationonline.org.uk
NATE: The National Association for the Teaching of English	www.nate.org.uk
Revision Guides	e.g. GCSE AQA English Language for the Grade 9-1 Course, published by CGP Books. (Note there are similar books for other awarding bodies such as OCR and Edexcel)
UKLA: United Kingdom Literacy Association	www.ukla.org

REFERENCES

Bond, B., Johnson, J., Patmore, M., Weiss, N. and Barker, G. (2018). *Getting into Teacher Training*. 3rd edition. London: Learning Matters.

DfE (2011). *Teachers' Standards*. London: HMSO.

DfE (2013). *National Curriculum*. London: HMSO.

DfE (2019a, Sept.). *Initial Teacher Training Core Content Framework*. London: HMSO.

DfE (2019b). 'Reducing workload: supporting teachers in the early stages of their career. Advice for school leaders, induction tutors, mentors and appropriate bodies'. Available at: https://core.ac.uk/reader/199234376 [Accessed 11 March 2021].

DfE (2019c). *Early Career Framework*. London: HMSO.

DfE (2020a, 4 Sept.). Initial Teacher Training (ITT): Criteria and supporting advice, section C1.3. London: HMSO.

PART 2

MATHEMATICS

INTRODUCTION TO THE MATHEMATICS SECTION

You need to consider whether your personal skills in mathematics meet the requirements specified by the DfE. These are:

> *Teachers should use data and graphs to interpret information, identify patterns and trends and draw appropriate conclusions. They need to interpret pupil data and understand statistics and graphs in the news, academic reports and relevant papers.*

> *Teachers should be able to complete mathematical calculations fluently with whole numbers, fractions, decimals and percentages. They should be able to solve mathematical problems using a variety of methods and approaches including: estimating and rounding, sense checking answers, breaking down problems into simpler steps and explaining and justifying answers using appropriate language.*

(DfE, 2020a)

Chapter 10 is an initial audit. It is intended to allow you to establish what you know, what you do not know and what you are unsure about. It is a formative step in clarifying your understanding and, with the other chapters, will help you identify those areas of mathematics where you are confident and those where you will need further consolidation. Each question in the audit is referenced to the appropriate chapter, where you will find notes and examples covering the basic ideas. In *Chapter 19*, at the end of the book, there are references which you can use to further develop your knowledge and understanding.

It is not possible to identify the number of questions that must have been answered correctly for a decision to be made about meeting the requirements: developing your mathematical confidence is not a tick box exercise. But as a guide if you are unable to answer the majority of the questions in each section you are unlikely to be meeting the requirements.

Following the audit, *Chapter 11* provides a short introduction to numbers and calculation but does not include any questions. *Chapters 12 to 16* cover the mathematical subject knowledge specified by the DfE as essential. Each of these chapters follows a similar format, providing an explanation of the appropriate knowledge supported by worked examples and then a set of questions for you to attempt. Answers and explanations for questions are to be found in *Chapter 17*. *Chapter 18* presents a glossary of mathematical terms.

Note: This symbol indicates that calculators should not be used:

This symbol indicates that calculators can be used:

10

INITIAL AUDIT

1. [Refer to Chapters 12 and 13]

   A single operation on a calculator could be '×10' or '×100' or '÷10', etc.

   Here are some pairs of numbers. Write down the single operation that would change the first number into the second number:

   (a) 50 000   505   (b) 9 090   909 000 000   (c) 4367   4.367

   (d) 7.49   749.0   (e) 1001   1 001 000   (f) 5.6   0.056

2. [Refer to Chapter 12]

   Trevor runs a sports club for primary school children. There are 96 children in the club. He divides the children into eight identical teams. In each team there are seven boys. How many girls are there in each team?

3. [Refer to Chapter 13]

   Work out $\dfrac{3}{4} + \dfrac{1}{8}$.

4. [Refer to Chapter 13]

   Metals are added to pure gold to produce different colours of gold.

   Green gold is a mixture of pure gold, silver and copper in the ratio, by weight, of $15:4:1$.

   A green gold ring weighs 4 g. What weight of this is pure gold?

5. [Refer to Chapter 13]

   Find the fraction which is exactly halfway between $3\dfrac{3}{4}$ and $\dfrac{3}{4}$.

6. [Refer to Chapter 13]

   The ratio of the volume of oil to the volume of vinegar in French dressing for salads is $3:1$.

   (a) How much vinegar must be added to 72 ml of oil to make some French dressing?

   (b) A chef needs to make a litre of French dressing.

   What volumes of oil and vinegar does the chef need?

7. [Refer to Chapter 13]

   In a survey, 400 people were questioned about recycling.

   (a) 75% of the people said they recycled.

   How many people was this?

   (b) $\frac{7}{10}$ of the people said they recycled bottles.

   How many people was this?

   (c) 120 of the people said they did not separate their glass bottles into different colours.

   Write 120 as a percentage of the total number of people surveyed.

8. [Refer to Chapter 12]

   A teacher plans to take a class of 30 pupils on a school trip. Here are the places the pupils could visit:

   (a) A zoo, 38 miles from school, entrance charge per pupil = £4

   (b) A museum, 30 miles from school, entrance charge per pupil = £6

   (c) A space science show, 20 miles from school, entrance charge per pupil = £12

   The coach company will charge £8 per mile.

   There are no entrance charges for teachers.

   Which is the cheapest trip and what is the difference between the most expensive and the cheapest trips?

9. [Refer to Chapter 14]

   Kai calculates $142\,378 \times 5239$ and gets the answer $74\,587\,642$.

   How could Kai tell that she has made a mistake?

10. [Refer to Chapter 13]

Put these fractions in order of size, starting with the smallest:

$\dfrac{11}{16}$, $\dfrac{1}{2}$, $\dfrac{5}{8}$, $\dfrac{15}{16}$ and $\dfrac{3}{4}$.

11. [Refer to Chapter 13]

Sarah bought a guitar which she later sold on the internet for £54.39.

She made a loss of 16%.

How much did the guitar originally cost?

12. [Refer to Chapters 12 and 13]

The table shows the number of tickets sold for a play.

	Number of tickets sold for each performance				
	Tues	Wed	Thurs	Fri	Sat
Full price	80	83	140	137	210
Concession	120	117	108	120	90
Total	200	200	248	257	300

Full price tickets cost £13.80 each. Concession tickets cost £8.50 each.

(a) Calculate the total income from ticket sales for Saturday's performance.

(b) What percentage of the tickets sold for Tuesday's performance were concessions?

(c) The total cost of putting on the play is £9787. The total income is £13 645.

Which of the following gives the closest estimate of the profit as a fraction of the total cost?

(i) $\dfrac{3}{10}$ (ii) $\dfrac{2}{5}$ (iii) $\dfrac{7}{10}$ (iv) $\dfrac{1}{2}$

13. [Refer to Chapter 14]

(a) Round 23.4649 to 2 decimal places.

(b) Round 23 458 925 to the nearest thousand.

(c) Round 4.7921 m to the nearest cm.

14. [Refer to Chapter 15]

These box and whisker diagrams compare the exam results for four maths classes in a school.

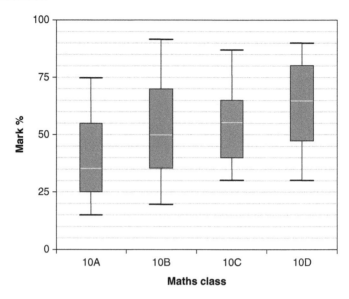

(a) Which class had the greatest range of marks?

(b) For which class was the median mark 35 marks above the lowest mark?

(c) What was the interquartile range for class 10A?

15. [Refer to Chapter 15]

This cumulative frequency graph shows time spent doing homework by students in a school's Year 11.

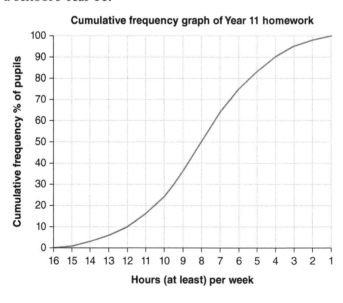

(a) What was the median time spent doing homework?

(b) There were 240 students in Year 11. How many students spent at least six hours per week doing homework?

16. [Refer to Chapter 15]

This scatter graph can be used to compare the performance of students in two tests. There were 23 students in the class. The straight line on the graph is a line showing equal scores on both tests.

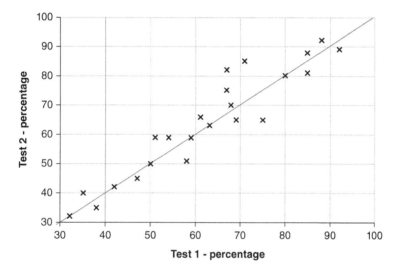

(a) How many students gained the same mark on both tests?

(b) How many students scored 80% or more in the 2nd test?

17. [Refer to Chapter 15]

A school has two football teams: Under 13s and Under 15s. The pie charts show information about the games each team won and lost last season. The Under 13s played 28 matches and the Under 15s played 18 matches. Which team won more matches?

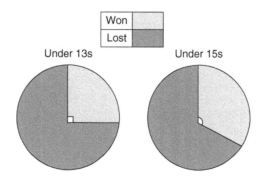

18. [Refer to Chapter 15]

    Calculate the mean, median and mode for this set of data:

    | 3.6 | 3.5 | 3.2 | 3.2 | 3.4 | 3.9 | 3.1 | 3.2 | 3.5 | 3.8 |

19. [Refer to Chapter 15]

    This table shows the Progress 8 scores for schools in two local authorities (LAs).

	Progress 8 scores				
LA 1	0.45	0.32	0.25	0.04	−0.24
LA 2	0.47	0.21	0.2	0.1	−1.2

    Would the mean or the median be the better average to use here for comparison? Give a reason for your decision.

20. [Refer to Chapter 16]

    Estimate the number of people in the world who are currently on their mobile phones.

21. [Refer to Chapters 13 and 16]

    In a test, Tom gets exactly 10 of the first 15 questions correct. He then answers all the remaining questions correctly. Tom has answered 80% of all the questions correctly.

    How many questions are there on the test?

22. [Refer to Chapter 13]

    A property developer sells two houses, each for £252000. Based on the prices he paid, he made a loss of 20% on one of the houses and a profit of 20% on the other. Overall, did he make a profit or a loss? Of how much?

23. [Refer to Chapter 15]

    A student takes five literacy tests and four numeracy tests.

    The scores she achieves in each test are shown in the table:

Test	1	2	3	4	5
Numeracy	61	59	64	72	
Literacy	59	68	63	62	63

(a) What is the difference in the mean scores for literacy and numeracy?

(b) She needs to achieve a mean score of 68 in numeracy. What mark must she gain in test 5 for numeracy in order to achieve this?

24. [Refer to Chapter 12]

A class assessment consists of a project and a written test. This formula is used to calculate a final mark.

$$\text{Final mark} = \frac{(\text{Project mark} \times 40)}{20} + \frac{(\text{Written mark} \times 60)}{40}$$

Calculate the final mark for a student who gained 12 marks for their project and 24 marks in the written test.

11

NUMBERS AND CALCULATION

Teachers should be able to complete mathematical calculations fluently with whole numbers, fractions, decimals and percentages

(DfE, 2020a)

a) TYPES OF NUMBER

The numbers we are most familiar with are the *positive whole numbers* {1, 2, 3, 4 ...} which we use for counting.

When we calculate with whole numbers, sometimes the answer is another positive whole number (for example, 4 + 6 = 10), but sometimes it is not. If we only had positive whole numbers, we would not be able to represent the answer to 3 – 5. We therefore also need the *negative whole numbers*, so that we can write 3 – 5 = –2.

When we divide one whole number by another, sometimes the answer is another whole number (18 ÷ 3 = 6), but sometimes it is not. If we only had positive and negative whole numbers, we would not be able to represent the answer to 5 ÷ 10. We therefore need *fractions and decimals* so that we can write 5 ÷ 10 = 0.5, or say that 5 is half of 10. We also need fractions and decimals to measure parts of a whole, or parts of a number or of a unit. For example, we might want to accurately measure a piece of wood that is more than 14 cm but less than 15 cm, so we need a way of representing the length of the extra bit, and for this we use fractions and decimals. For example, we might say that the piece of wood measures 14.25 cm or $14\frac{1}{4}$ cm.

Percentages are fractions out of 100, so 62% is another way of writing 62 out of 100 or $\frac{62}{100}$. Percentages are, therefore, just another way of representing a fraction (or a decimal).

There are other types of number which, as a teacher, you will not be expected to know about unless you teach mathematics at KS3 or above. For example, π (pronounced pi) is a number used in geometry and advanced mathematics which cannot be represented exactly using fractions or decimals, although it is sometimes approximated as 3.142 or $\frac{22}{7}$. Another example is $\sqrt{2}$ (the square root of 2, or the number which multiplied by itself gives the answer 2). Again, this number cannot be represented exactly by a fraction or a decimal.

b) THE DECIMAL SYSTEM

In everyday life, we use the decimal system to write numbers. The word 'decimal' comes from the Latin words 'decem' meaning ten, and 'decimus' meaning tenth. In the decimal system of writing numbers, the place values are all related to powers of 10. It is important to remember this if you want to understand why our methods of calculation work, rather than just following rules.

Below is part of a decimal place value table and shows the representation of the number 452.7

Thousands (10^3)	Hundreds (10^2)	Tens (10^1)	Units (10^0)		Tenths $\frac{1}{10^1}$	Hundredths $\frac{1}{10^2}$	Thousandths $\frac{1}{10^3}$
	4	5	2	.	7		

This is telling us that 452.7 = 4 hundreds + 5 tens + 2 units or ones + 7 tenths.

Which is the same as saying $452.7 = 4 \times 10^2 + 5 \times 10^1 + 2 \times 10^0 + 7 \times \frac{1}{10^1}$

Or alternatively, that $452.7 = 400 + 50 + 2 + \frac{7}{10}$.

So, when we write a number in the decimal system, we are splitting it up into powers of 10.

[Units, or ones, are multiples of 10^0. If you wonder why $10^0 = 1$, you can look it up or ask one of your peers who is teaching maths.]

c) TYPES OF CALCULATION

There are four different types of calculation that you are expected to be able to do when working with whole numbers, fractions, decimals and percentages: addition (+), subtraction (−), multiplication (×), and division (÷). And there are three different ways in which you might have to do these calculations: mentally, with a pen and paper, or with a calculator. These are discussed in the next chapter.

12

CALCULATING WITH WHOLE NUMBERS

Teachers should be able to complete mathematical calculations fluently with whole numbers

(DfE, 2020a)

a) ADDITION WITH WHOLE NUMBERS

Using pen and paper, we do 'column addition' where we write the numbers underneath one another in columns.

There are two main ways of thinking about column addition.

Standard addition method for 45 + 38		
Step 1	(Looking at the units column) 5 + 8 = 13 = 10 + 3 'put down the 3 and carry the 1 (ten)'	45 +38 ₁3
Step 2	(Looking at the tens column) 4 + 3 = 7 add 1 (the carry 1) = 8 So the answer is 83	45 +38 8₁3

OR

Tens first method for 45 + 38		
Step 1	(Looking at the tens column) 40 + 30 = 70 We say '4 + 3 = 7'	45 +38 70

Tens first method for 45 + 38 (continued)		
Step 2	(Looking at the units column) 5 + 8 = 13 Write this underneath the 70	45 +38 70 13
Step 3	Repeat the method adding 70 and 13, i.e. 7 + 1 = 8 (in the tens column) 0 + 3 = 3 (in the units column) So, the answer is 83	45 +38 70 13 83

When doing mental addition, some people do column addition in their heads. Other people visualise a number line. They might work out 33 + 49 as:

Another way of doing 33 + 49 as a mental calculation is to make the numbers easier by thinking $33 + 49 = 33 + 50 - 1 = 83 - 1 = 82$

b) SUBTRACTION WITH WHOLE NUMBERS

Using pen and paper, we do 'column subtraction'.

There are two main ways of thinking about column subtraction. You will probably be more familiar with the decomposition method.

Decomposition method for 63 − 35		
Step 1	(Looking at the units column) 3 − 5 (can't do it without going negative) So, change 63 into 50 + 13, writing 1 near the 3 (units) and 5 near the 6 (tens) You may know this as 'borrowing' a ten from the 60 and adding it to the 3	$^56^13$ −35
Step 2	13 − 5 = 8 Write 8 in the units column	$^56^13$ −35 8

(Continued)

(Continued)

Decomposition method for 63 – 35		
Step 3	50 – 30 = 20 Usually said as '5 – 3 = 2' Write 2 in the tens column So, the answer is 28	$^56^13$ –35 28

For 502 – 37 the method works like this:

Decomposition method for 502 – 37		
Step 1	2 – 7 (can't do it without going negative) So, change 500 + 2 into 490 + 12, writing 4 near the 5, 9 near the 0 and 1 near the 2 You may know this as 'borrowing' a hundred from the 5, adding it to the 0, then 'borrowing' a ten from the 100 and adding it to the 2.	$^45^90^12$ – 37
Step 2	12 – 7 = 5 Write 5 in the units column	$^45^90^12$ – 3 7 5
Step 3	9 – 3 = 6 Write 6 in the tens column	$^45^90^12$ – 3 7 6 5
Step 4	Write 4 in the hundreds column So, the answer is 465	$^45^90^12$ – 3 7 4 6 5

The second method is equal addition. This method relies on the fact that the difference between two numbers remains the same if the same number is added to both of those numbers. So, the answer to 63 – 35 is the same as the answer to 73 – 45 or 83 – 55, and so on.

Equal addition method for 63 – 35		
Step 1	3 – 5 (can't do it without going negative) So, change 60 + 3 into 60 + 13 We have added 10 to the top number so we need to add 10 to the bottom number to keep the difference the same. This becomes 40 + 5	60 + ^{13} ^{4}30 + 5

Equal addition method for 63 – 35 (continued)		
Step 2	13 – 5 = 8 Write 8 in the units column 60 – 40 = 20 Write 20 in the tens column	$60 + {}^1 3$ ${}^4\cancel{3}0 + 5$ ——— $20 + 8$
Step 3	20 + 8 = 28	

For 502 – 37 the method works like this:

Equal addition method for 502 – 37		
Step 1	2 – 7 (can't do it without going negative) So, change 500 + 2 into 500 + 12 We have added 10 to the top number so we need to add 10 to the bottom number to keep the difference the same. This becomes 40 + 7	$500 + {}^1 2$ ${}^4\cancel{3}0 + 7$ ——— $460 + 5$
Step 2	12 – 7 = 5 Write 5 in the units column 500 – 40 = 460 Write 460 in the hundreds column	$500 + {}^1 2$ ${}^4\cancel{3}0 + 7$ ——— $460 + 5$
Step 3	460 + 5 = 465	

There are more mental methods for subtraction than for addition. For example, to calculate 63 – 35 you might

- Make the numbers easier:

  e.g. 63 – 35 = 63 – 40 + 5

  = 23 + 5

  = 28

Or

  63 – 35 = 63 – 33 – 2

  = 30 – 2

  = 28

- Count on:

Counting back 35 from 63 is difficult, but counting on from 35 to 63 is easier. This is called the 'shopkeeper's method' as it is how shopkeepers used to count as they gave change, before electronic tills.

35 to 40 = 5

40 to 60 = 20

60 to 63 = 3

then 5 + 20 + 3 = 28

- Use the same ideas but on a mental number line, starting at 63:

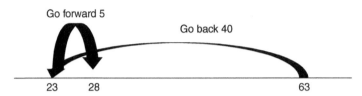

Or

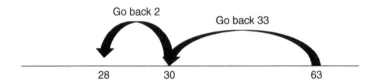

Or, starting at 35

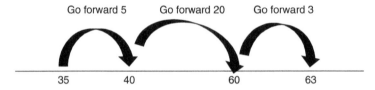

c) MULTIPLICATION WITH WHOLE NUMBERS

There are many ways of doing multiplication. We will give the formal method and the grid method here, as both are commonly taught.

Formal method for 87 × 36		
We are going to work out 6 lots of 87 and 30 lots of 87 and add them together.		
Step 1	Start by multiplying 87 by 6: Looking at the units column: 6 × 7 = 42 Write the 2 in the units column and 'carry' the 4 (representing 4 tens) into the tens column. Multiply the 6 by 8 (actually 80): 6 × 8 = 48. Add the 4 carried over, giving 52 (actually we are adding 480 and 40 together giving 520)	8 7 ×3 6 ――― 52₄2

	Formal method for 87 × 36 (continued)	
Step 2	Now multiply 87 by 30. Put a 0 as a place holder in the units column, as we are really multiplying by 30 not by 3. Looking at the tens column: $3 \times 7 = 21$. Put 1 in the tens column and carry the 2 into the hundreds column. $8 \times 3 = 24$, add the 2 carried over giving 26	$\begin{array}{r} 8\,7 \\ \times 3\ 6 \\ \hline 52_4 2 \\ 26_2 10 \end{array}$
Step 3	Add the 522 and the 2610 together, giving 3132.	$\begin{array}{r} 8\,7 \\ \times 3\ 6 \\ \hline 52_4 2 \\ 26_2 10 \\ \hline 3_1 1\ 32 \end{array}$

For larger numbers, the method can be continued:

e.g. for 469×72

$$
\begin{array}{rrrrr}
 & & 4 & 6 & 9 \\
\times & & & 7 & 2 \\
\hline
 & & 9 & 3 & 8 \\
3 & 2 & 8 & 3 & 0 \\
\hline
3 & 3 & 7 & 6 & 8 \\
\hline
\end{array}
$$

Note that for 72×469, although the answer is of course the same, the intermediate calculations are different:

$$
\begin{array}{rrrrr}
 & & & 7 & 2 \\
\times & & 4 & 6 & 9 \\
\hline
 & & 6 & 4 & 8 \\
 & 4 & 3 & 2 & 0 \\
2 & 8 & 8 & 0 & 0 \\
\hline
3 & 3 & 7 & 6 & 8 \\
\hline
\end{array}
$$

With the grid method, instead of doing 6×87 and 30×87 and adding the answers (as in the formal method), we now break the numbers down further and do 30×80, 6×80, 30×7 and 6×7 and add the answers.

×	30	6	Total
80	2400	480	2880
7	210	42	252
	2610	522	3132

For larger calculations, the grid can be expanded.

e.g. for 469×72:

×	400	60	9	Total
70	28 000	4200	630	32 830
2	800	120	18	938
	28 800	4320	648	33 768

For most multiplications, we would use a written method or a calculator. However, some easier multiplications can be done mentally.

For example, to calculate 39×5, we could adjust the numbers:

(i) We could double the five and then halve the answer:

$39 \times 10 = 390$

$390 \div 2 = 195$

Or

(ii) we could find 40 lots of 5 and then subtract a 5:

$40 \times 5 = 200$

$200 - 5 = 195$

d) DIVISION WITH WHOLE NUMBERS

There are two closely related formal written methods for division: long division and short division.

Long division for 735 ÷ 4		
Step 1	Starting with the hundreds, how many 4s in 7? (really, how many times will 4 go into 700?) Answer 1 (hundred); write down 1 in the hundreds column on top $1 \times 4 = 4$ so subtract 4 from 7 (really 400 from 700) to see what is left. 'Bring down' 3 (really 30) from the 735	$\begin{array}{r} 1 \\ 4\overline{)735} \\ -4 \\ \hline 33 \end{array}$

	Long division for 735 ÷ 4 (continued)	
Step 2	How many 4s in 33? (really, how many times will 4 go into 330?) Answer 8 (tens). Put 8 in the tens column on top 8 × 4 = 32 so subtract 32 from 33. 'Bring' down 5 from the 735.	$\begin{array}{r} 1\ 8 \\ 4\overline{)735} \\ -4 \\ \hline 33 \\ -32 \\ \hline 15 \end{array}$
Step 3	How many 4s in 15? Answer 3 3 × 4 = 12 so we have a remainder of 3 The answer is 183 remainder 3	$\begin{array}{r} 183 \quad \text{rem}3 \\ 4\overline{)735} \\ -4 \\ \hline 33 \\ -32 \\ \hline 15 \\ -12 \\ \hline 3 \end{array}$

Sometimes we want to continue the division to a number of decimal places. In this case we write 735 as 735.000... and continue the method, bringing down the zeros:

Step 4	Bring down the 0 from the 735.000... How many 4s in 30? Answer 7. Put 7 after the decimal point to get 183.7 7 × 4 = 28 so subtract 28 from 30 ... and so on, to as many decimal places as required.	$\begin{array}{r} 183.7 \\ 4\overline{)735.000...} \\ -4 \\ \hline 33 \\ -32 \\ \hline 15 \\ -12 \\ \hline 30 \\ 28 \\ \hline 2 \end{array}$

Short division is essentially the same as long division but we record the method differently. Many people find this quicker.

	Short division for 735 ÷ 4	
Step 1	Starting with the hundreds, how many 4s in 7? (really, how many times will 4 go into 700?) Answer 1 (hundred); write down 1 in the hundreds column on top	$\begin{array}{r} 1 \\ 4\overline{)7^335} \end{array}$

(Continued)

(Continued)

Short division for 735 ÷ 4		
	1 × 4 = 4 so subtract 4 from 7 (really 400 from 700) to see what is left, which is 3 (hundred) Carry the 3 forward by writing it in front of the next number	
Step 2	How many 4s in 33? (really, how many times will 4 go into 330?) Answer 8 (tens). Put 8 in tens column on top 8 × 4 = 32 so subtract 32 from 33 to see what is left. Carry the 1 forward	$\begin{array}{r} 1\ \ 8 \\ 4\overline{)\ 7\ ^3 3\ ^1 5} \end{array}$
Step 3	How many 4s in 15? Answer 3 3 × 4 = 12 so we have a remainder of 3 The answer is 183 remainder 3	$\begin{array}{r} 1\ \ 8\ \ 3 \qquad \text{rem} 3 \\ 4\overline{)\ 7\ ^3 3\ ^1 5} \end{array}$

As with long division, if we want the answer to a number of decimal places, we write 735 as 735.000... and continue the method.

Division is almost always done with a written method or with a calculator rather than mentally, unless the numbers are very straightforward, e.g. 18 ÷ 3 or 4523 ÷ 1000.

e) BIDMAS AND USING THE CALCULATOR

So far, we have looked at +, −, × and ÷ separately, but in real life we often need to combine these operations and we often use a calculator. It is important to follow the correct order of operations and to use the calculator correctly.

You may remember the acronym BIDMAS from school or college.

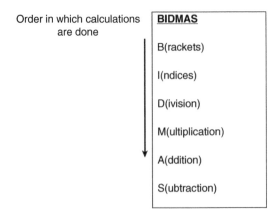

For example, suppose three friends go for a meal and split the bill equally. Their meals cost £16, £20 and £15. So, to calculate how much they each pay we need to calculate (16 + 20 + 15) ÷ 3 = 51 ÷ 3 = 17, so they each pay £17.

But if we enter 16 + 20 + 15 ÷ 3 into a calculator, we get the answer 41, which is not the answer we want. This happens because the calculator follows BIDMAS and does the division 15 ÷ 3 = 5 first before doing the addition, hence 16 + 20 + 5 = 41.

To avoid this, we can use brackets when entering the numbers into the calculator: (16 + 20 + 15) ÷ 3. This forces the calculator to work out the bracket first (that is, to find the total bill) and then to do the division.

Alternatively, we can enter 16 + 20 + 15 = to get the total 51 and then ÷ the 51 by 3.

Another example: Suppose I owe £100. I pay back £25 at the end of the first month and £18 at the end of the second month. How much do I still owe? I have paid back a total of 25 + 18 = 43 so I owe 100 − (25 + 18) = 100 − 43 = 57 so I still owe £57.

But if we enter 100 − 25 + 18 we get the answer 93, which is not the answer we want. Why does the calculator not do the addition 25 + 18 first and then the subtraction as dictated by BIDMAS? Surely addition gets done before subtraction? The answer is that addition and subtraction can actually be done in either order so, faced with a string of additions and subtractions, the calculator just works from left to right.

To avoid this, we can use brackets and enter 100 − (25 + 18) to force the calculator to evaluate the bracket first. Or we can enter 25 + 18 = to get 43 and then enter 100 − 43 =

Or we can enter 100 − 25 − 18 to get the answer 57.

A similar problem applies to multiplication and division which can also be done in either order. Suppose we want to do the calculation 1000 ÷ (20 × 5) to get the answer 10. BIDMAS suggests that division will be done before the multiplication, but we need to use brackets to force the calculator to do this. If we do not use brackets, it will tell us that 1000 ÷ 20 × 5 = 250, because faced with a string of multiplications and divisions, the calculator will work from left to right.

In a maths exam, you may have been asked to calculate something abstract like 15 − 3 × 4 and be expected to apply BIDMAS to get the right answer (3 not 48). But in real life, when you want to work something out, you will always know the context and what order it makes sense to do the calculations in. Calculators are very good at sums but do not understand the context you are working in, so you need to tell them exactly what to do by using brackets or entering parts of the calculation separately and then putting them together.

f) QUESTIONS IN CONTEXT

It is important to know how to do basic calculations without a calculator, but it is just as important to know which calculations you need to do. It could be argued that this is the most important skill, as most of us have access to a calculator most of the time, even if only on our phones. Faced with a question, we need to be able to identify the calculations that are required. There may be different ways to approach a calculation: for example $4 + 4 + 4$ is the same as 3×4 and $11 - (3 + 2)$ is the same as $11 - 3 - 2$.

QUESTIONS

1. (a) $246 + 3142$ (b) $3142 - 2718$ (c) 3208×15

   (d) $713 \div 23$ (e) $15\overline{)2145}$

2. Tinned tomatoes are packed in boxes. Each box holds 18 tins. The boxes are packed onto pallets. Each pallet holds 36 boxes. The pallets are packed into containers. Each container holds 14 pallets. How many tins are there in a full container?

3. 366 pupils are going by coach on a school trip. There must be one adult for every 12 pupils.

   (a) How many passengers will be travelling on the coaches?

   Each coach has 53 seats.

   (b) How many coaches will be needed?

4. The milometer on a van shows 103 827 at the start of the day and 104 301 at the end of the day. How many miles did the van travel that day?

5. A ream of photocopying paper (500 sheets) is approximately 5 cm thick. What is the approximate thickness of one sheet of paper in millimetres?

6. A teacher is planning a visit to an activity centre with a group of students. They will use the school minibus.

The round trip is approximately 200 miles. The fuel consumption for the minibus is 32 miles per gallon. The minibus uses diesel fuel which costs £1.19 per litre.

1 gallon = 4.546 litres

What is the estimated fuel cost for the visit? Give your answer to the nearest pound.

7. Find the correct operation (+, −, ×, ÷) that belongs in each ◯ to make the following statements true:

(a) (37 ◯ 21) ◯ 223 = 1000   (b) 27 ◯ (36 ◯ 18) = 675

(c) 476 ◯ (2040 ◯ 24) = 391   (d) (720 ◯ 340) ◯ 42 ◯ 20 = 798

8. Find a route from START to FINISH that totals 100 exactly.

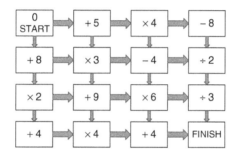

9. This table shows some data about state-funded primary and secondary schools.

		2015/16	2016/17	2017/18	2018/19	2019/20
State-funded primary	Number of schools	16 778	16 786	16 766	16 769	16 784
	Headcount total	4 615 172	4 689 658	4 716 244	4 727 089	4 714 722
State-funded secondary	Number of schools	3401	3408	3436	3448	3456
	Headcount total	3 193 418	3 223 089	3 258 451	3 327 970	3 409 277

(DfE, 2020b)

(a) How many more primary and secondary pupils were there in 2019/20 compared with 2015/16?

(b) Dividing the total headcount by the number of schools gives the average number of students per school. For secondary schools is the average in 2019/20 higher, lower or the same compared with the average 2015/16?

10. In a mock GCSE examination, a student's mark for each of the three papers will be added to give the total final mark. The table shows the minimum mark needed to gain a pass at each grade.

	8	7	6	5	4
Minimum Total mark	340	300	260	220	200

A student's mark for paper 1 was 65; her mark for paper 2 was 75.

What mark does she need to gain on paper 3 in order to gain a pass at grade 6?

11. The estimated cost of poor numeracy for the UK is £388 million per week.

(a) Estimate the annual cost.

(b) Estimate the daily cost.

12. A student achieved the following marks in three tests, test A, test B and test C.

Test	A	B	C
Raw mark	70	30	12

The final weighted score is calculated using this formula:

$$\text{weighted score} = \frac{(A \times 60)}{100} + \frac{(B \times 30)}{100} + C$$

Calculate the student's weighted score.

13

FRACTIONS, DECIMALS, PERCENTAGES (INCLUDING RATIO AND PROPORTION)

Teachers should be able to complete mathematical calculations fluently with whole numbers, fractions, decimals and percentages.

(DfE, 2020a)

a) PROPORTION

A 'proportion' is a number considered in comparative relation to a whole. Fractions, decimals, percentages, and ratio are different ways of expressing proportion or parts of a whole.

These diagrams show the section of the number line between 0 and 1 and how it may be divided up into four equal parts using fractions, decimals and percentages. The diagrams demonstrate the equivalences between fractions, decimals and percentages.

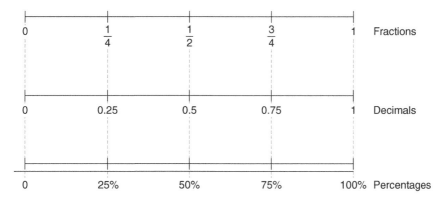

Ratios are presented slightly differently but can be interpreted as fractions (or as decimals or percentages).

In the following explanations you will need to remember that a factor is a number that will divide into another number. For example, 3 is a factor of 6; 2 is a factor of 10; 5 is *not* a factor of 11.

b) FRACTIONS

If p and q are whole numbers, then $\frac{p}{q}$ is called a fraction. So $\frac{3}{5}$ is an example of a fraction. If we replace each number with a dot like this, $\div$, then you will recognise the symbol for division. This is where the division symbol comes from: $\frac{3}{5}$ means $3 \div 5$.

In fact, a fraction can be presented or interpreted in several different ways. All these are equivalent, but they may seem different, and this is why fractions can be a bit confusing.

(i) A fraction can be thought of as the result of dividing a shape into equal parts and taking one or more of those parts. For example, $\frac{3}{5}$ can be represented as

This is usually the first way people are taught to interpret fractions at school.

(ii) A fraction can be thought of as the result of dividing a whole number into equal parts and taking one or more of those parts, so instead of being parts of a shape, the fraction $\frac{3}{5}$ can be three-fifths of a number. For example, if $\frac{3}{5}$ of a year group of 200 pupils are boys then to find the number of boys, we divide 200 by 5 to get one-fifth, and then multiply by 3 to get three-fifths. $200 \div 5 = 40$ and $40 \times 3 = 120$. So there are 120 boys in the year group.

(iii) A fraction can indicate a division. The fraction $\frac{3}{5}$ can mean $3 \div 5$ and this is how we convert a fraction into a decimal. As a 'paper calculation':

$$\begin{array}{r} 0.6 \\ 5\overline{)3.^30} \end{array}$$

5 into 3 doesn't go, (goes '0' times); there is a 'carry over' (a remainder) of 3. 5 into 30 goes 6. So $\frac{3}{5} = 0.6$ (notice that the decimal points in the division ought to 'line up').

(iv) A fraction is a number and can be represented on a number line.

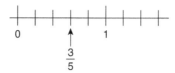

Here, we have split the number line between 0 and 1 into five equal parts and counted along to the third one. So we have taken $\frac{3}{5}$ of the number 1.

(v) $\frac{3}{5}$ can be a comparison between part of a set and the whole set.

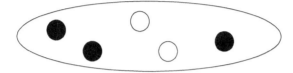

Here, $\frac{3}{5}$ of the dots are black. Notice that we could also say that the ratio of black dots to white dots is 3:2 (not 3:5; this would be the proportion of dots which are black).

(vi) $\frac{3}{5}$ can be a comparison between two sets of objects or measurements.

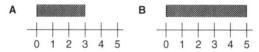

The length of A is $\frac{3}{5}$ the length of B. Here, the ratio of lengths A:B is 3:5

Equivalent fractions are formed by multiplying or dividing both the numerator (top number) and the denominator (bottom number) of a fraction by the same number. For example:

$\frac{3}{5} = \frac{6}{10}$ multiplying the numerator and denominator by 2.

$\frac{9}{15} = \frac{3}{5}$ dividing the numerator and denominator by 3 which is a 'common' factor of both 9 and 15. This is called cancelling. If an answer requires a fraction in its simplest form, this means using the smallest whole numbers possible and you may need to cancel.

Improper fractions are fractions where the numerator is larger than the denominator. (These are sometimes called 'top-heavy' fractions.) For example: $\frac{7}{4}$ or $\frac{9}{5}$. These fractions represent numbers that are greater than 1.

Mixed numbers are numbers with a whole number part and a fraction. For example: $1\frac{2}{5}$ or $3\frac{1}{4}$ By dividing the numerator by the denominator, an improper fraction can be written as a mixed number, so $\frac{7}{4}$ would be written as $1\frac{3}{4}$ and $\frac{9}{5}$ would be written as $1\frac{4}{5}$

Fractions can be added and subtracted (and also multiplied and divided, but you are less likely to need to do this). You will more often need to find a fraction of a quantity.

ADDITION AND SUBTRACTION OF FRACTIONS

To add (or subtract) two fractions which have the same denominator is intuitive. For example, $\frac{3}{7}+\frac{1}{7}=\frac{4}{7}$ and $\frac{3}{7}-\frac{1}{7}=\frac{2}{7}$. But what if we want to add or subtract fractions with different denominators, for example $\frac{3}{7}$ and $\frac{1}{5}$? The answer is to use equivalent fractions each with a denominator of 35 (from 7×5). This turns the calculations into $\frac{15}{35}+\frac{7}{35}=\frac{22}{35}$ and $\frac{15}{35}-\frac{7}{35}=\frac{8}{35}$

FINDING A FRACTION OF A QUANTITY

This is fairly intuitive. For example, to find $\frac{1}{8}$ of 240, calculate $240 \div 8 = 30$; then to find $\frac{3}{8}$ of 240, calculate $30 \times 3 = 90$. (Look back at section (ii) above for another example.)

If you have a scientific calculator, you can use it to input fractions and calculate with them directly. Use the fraction button ⊟ or [a b/c] to input a fraction. If your calculator uses [a b/c], the fraction/mixed number will appear written as, for example, 3⌐8 or 2⌐3⌐8 rather than $\frac{3}{8}$ or $2\frac{3}{8}$.

Alternatively, you can just use the calculator to calculate $3 \div 8 = 0.375$ and then do the decimal calculation $0.375 \times 240 = 90$.

c) DECIMALS

Decimals are a different way of representing fractions that are 'out of a power of ten'. That is, fractions that have 10 or 100 or 1000 or a higher power of 10 as their denominator.

Because the first number after the decimal point represents tenths, 0.4 is equivalent to $\frac{4}{10}$ (or $\frac{2}{5}$). Because the second number after the decimal point represents hundredths, 0.56 is equivalent to $\frac{56}{100}$ (which is equivalent to $\frac{28}{50}$ or $\frac{14}{25}$). These two decimals are shown on the place value table below.

Hundreds	Tens	Units		Tenths	Hundredths	Thousandths
		0	.	4		
		0	.	5	6	

Calculating with decimal numbers using a written or mental method is the same as calculating with whole numbers, with the added complication that you need to get the decimal point in the right place.

Addition and subtraction of decimal numbers: The key to success here is to ensure that the numbers are written so that the place values line up. In other words, ensure that the decimal points are in line. So to add 3.62 and 17.9:

```
          3  .  6   2
   +   1  7  .  9  (0)
      ─────────────────
       2  1  .  5   2
       1  1
```

Multiplication of decimal numbers: It is easiest to forget the decimal points, do the multiplication and then use one of two methods to position the decimal point. You can either count from right to left the total number of decimal places in the question and put in the decimal point, or use estimation to obtain the correct size of the answer.

So to do 5.34×0.6, calculate $534 \times 6 = 3204$. There are three decimal places altogether in the question (the 3, the 4 and the 6) so the answer is 3.204. Or, by estimation, the answer must be less than 5.34 but more than half of 5.34 because 0.6 is less than 1 and more than 0.5. So, the answer must be 3.204.

Division of decimal numbers: When dividing, whole numbers are much easier to work with than decimal ones, so use an equivalent fraction with whole numbers. For example, to work out $6 \div 0.4$, write it as $\frac{6}{0.4}$. Then, multiplying both numbers by 10 to get an equivalent fraction gives $\frac{60}{4}$ which is 15.

Note: Some fractions, such as $\frac{5}{8}$, convert to decimals which stop. For example, $\frac{5}{8} = 0.625$. These are called terminating decimals. Other fractions, such as $\frac{1}{3} = 0.33333...$ convert to decimals which just keep on repeating. These are called recurring decimals. Examples of other common fractions which produce recurring decimals are: $\frac{2}{3}, \frac{1}{6}, \frac{5}{12}$

Dots are used to show that a decimal recurs. If only one digit recurs, a dot is placed over that digit the first time it occurs after the decimal place. For example, 0.1666666... is written as $0.1\dot{6}$ and 3.3333... is written as $3.\dot{3}$. If a group of digits recurs, a dot is placed over the first and last digits in the group. For example 0.013713713713... is written as $0.0\dot{1}3\dot{7}$.

There is a third group of decimals which neither repeat nor recur. For example, the decimal forms of π and $\sqrt{2}$ go on for ever with non-repeating strings of decimals.

d) PERCENTAGES

Percent means 'out of 100' or 'per hundred'. When you use percentages, the quantity has been divided into 100 parts. The percentage tells you how many of these parts you have, so 5% means 5 parts out of 100 or $5 \div 100$ or $\frac{5}{100}$ which can also be written as 0.05; 75% represents $75 \div 100$ or $\frac{75}{100}$, and can be written as 0.75 (think of percentages as decimals in disguise, so 38% = 0.38). If you are working out percentages mentally or on paper, it is often easier to find 10% (by dividing by 10) or 1% (by dividing by 100) and then multiply that answer as required. For example, to find 30% of 40, find 10%, which is 4, and multiply by 3 to get 12. Or, to find 7% of 240, find 1%, which is 2.4 and multiply by 7 to get 16.8.

Calculating with percentages is easy if you remember that they are just fractions with denominators of 100.

Calculating % of a quantity: For example, to find 45% of £62, calculate

$$\frac{45}{100} \times 62 = (45 \div 100) \times 62$$

$$= 27.9$$

Some people prefer to find 1% and then multiply by 45:

$$\frac{62}{100} \times 45 = (62 \div 100) \times 45$$

$$= 27.9$$

Whichever method is used, 45% of £62 is £27.90.

Sometimes we need to compare two percentages. For example, which is larger, 45% of 62 or 35% of 80? We use the same method for each calculation and then compare the answers. Notice that here, although 45% is larger than 35%, 45% of 62 (= 27.9) is smaller than 35% of 80 (= 28) so we cannot just compare the percentages.

Calculating % increase or decrease: To increase £62 by 45%, we find 45% of £62 as before and then add it on. 62 + 27.9 = 89.9.

An alternative method is to say that the answer will be 145% of 62 and to calculate

$$(145 \div 100) \times 62 = 1.45 \times 62 = 89.9$$

Whichever method is used, the answer is £89.90.

Calculating one number as a % of another: To find what percentage 30 is of 75, we first write it as the fraction $\dfrac{30}{75}$ and then convert this to a percentage:

$$(30 \div 75) \times 100 = 40$$

So the answer is 40%.

Calculating a % change: The method is best illustrated with an example.

The number of students in a school increases from 1200 to 1350. What is the percentage increase?

Find the actual increase then divide this by the original amount and change the resulting fraction into a percentage. Here, the actual increase = 150 so the fraction is $\dfrac{150}{1200}$ then

$$\dfrac{150}{1200} \times 100\% = 12.5\%$$

Reverse percentages: Beware!

A coat is reduced in a sale by 75% to £50. What was the original price of the coat?

It is tempting to find 75% of 50 and add it on, giving us £137.50, but this would be wrong. In fact, the price of the coat is now 25% of the original price, so 1% of the original is £50 ÷ 25 = £2 and 100% of the original price is £2 × 100 = £200. You can check by finding 75% of £200 (= £150 reduction), so the sale price is indeed £50. Think about increasing £1000 by 100% so it doubles to £2000. If you then tried to reduce £2000 by 100% you would get to zero, not back to £1000. You need to reduce £2000 by 50% to get to £1000.

e) CONVERTING BETWEEN FRACTIONS, DECIMALS AND PERCENTAGES

You will have noticed that when doing calculations, we often find it useful to convert between fractions, decimals and percentages. Here is a summary of how to do this.

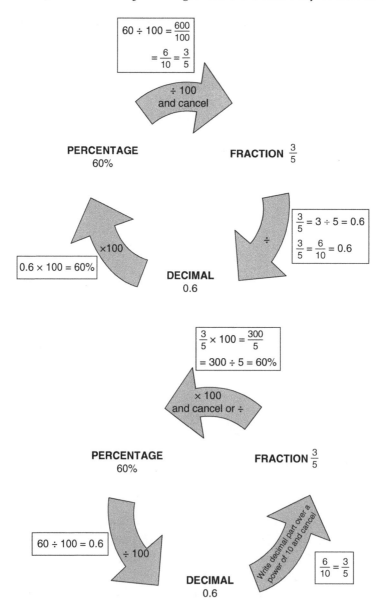

f) RATIO AND PROPORTION

A ratio is used to compare two or more quantities. Think of ratio as a way of comparing 'part' to 'part'. For example, if a drink is made using juice and water in the ratio 1:4 it means that for every litre of juice used, 4 litres of water are added. Note that it doesn't matter what units you are using. What matters is that the units are the same. Here the ratio could be 1 gallon of juice to 4 gallons of water, but not 1 gallon of juice to 4 litres of water.

Ratios can be simplified in the same way as fractions. For example, 2:5 is the same ratio as 4:10 or 100:250.

Splitting an amount in a given ratio: To split £200 in the ratio 2:3 we need to first split it into 2 + 3 = 5 equal parts: 200 ÷ 5 = 40. Then we calculate 2 × 40 and 3 × 40 to get the answers £80 and £120. Then check that £80 + £120 add to £200, which they do.

Calculating a total: If juice and water are mixed in the ratio 2:5 to make a drink, then if we have 4 litres of juice, we need (4 ÷ 2) × 5 = 10 litres of water and we can make 4 + 10 = 14 litres of drink.

Ratio and proportion are sometimes confused. Ratio compares part to part while proportion compares part to whole. Ratio uses the notation $p:q$ where p and q are whole numbers. Proportions can be written as fractions, decimals or percentages. For example: Suppose that in a class of 32 pupils, 18 are boys and 14 are girls.

Then the **ratio** of boys to girls is 18:14 which simplifies to 9:7.

The **proportion** of boys in the class is $\dfrac{18}{32} = \dfrac{9}{16}$ or 0.5625 or 56.25%

QUESTIONS

1. Write:

   (a) 0.4 as a fraction and a percentage

   (b) $\dfrac{7}{10}$ as a decimal and a percentage

   (c) 36% as a fraction and a decimal

   (d) 0.59 as a fraction and a percentage

   (e) $\dfrac{27}{100}$ as a decimal and a percentage

   (f) 17% as a fraction and a decimal

2. Find:

   (a) 15% of £60   (b) 65% of 240   (c) $\dfrac{3}{8}$ of 500 cm

   (d) $\dfrac{4}{7}$ of 154   (e) 0.8 × 32   (f) 0.65 × 144

3.

    (a) Find the fraction exactly halfway between $\frac{2}{5}$ and $\frac{3}{5}$

    (b) Find any fraction that lies between $\frac{3}{10}$ and $\frac{1}{3}$

4. The table below shows the number of students who start and finish three courses in a 6th form college. Calculate the retention rates for each subject.

The retention rate is defined as the percentage of students who complete a course.

Course	Number of students	
	at start of course	at end of course
English	123	98
History	157	123
Psychology	132	105

5. In a primary school with 450 pupils, two-thirds qualify for free school meals. In another primary school with 300 pupils, half qualify for free school meals.

    (a) How many pupils qualify altogether?

    (b) What fraction is this of the total number of pupils?

6. A textbook is priced at £9.50. From one supplier it is on offer for £8.75. From another supplier it is on offer with a 20% discount. Which is the better buy?

7. Write these numbers in order, starting with the smallest.

    3.47 $3\frac{53}{100}$ 3.1 $3\frac{8}{10}$ 3.29

8. A primary school has a weekly lesson time of 23.5 hours. Pupils do 5 hours of maths each week.

What percentage of the weekly lesson time is spent on mathematics? Give your answer to the nearest percent.

9. Year 9 students were asked to opt for either swimming or tennis. Their choices are shown in this table.

	Swimming	Tennis
Girls	27	33
Boys	42	28

(a) What percentage of the students who went swimming were girls?

(b) What percentage of girls chose tennis?

(c) What percentage of all students chose swimming?

10. In a football competition, the allocation of tickets between the home club and the away club is in the ratio $6:1$

(a) For one match there are 28000 tickets. How many should each club receive?

(b) Clifton Wanderers are playing at home. They receive 21600 tickets. How many tickets does the away team receive?

(c) Trent are playing away. They receive 2500 tickets. How many tickets do their opponents get?

11. This table shows the GCSE grades in mathematics achieved by a school's Y11 students for the period 2017 to 2019.

Grade	9	8	7	6	5	4	3 and below	Total number of students
2017	2	8	14	25	62	67	31	209
2018	3	10	22	22	73	37	21	188
2019	4	7	31	46	43	46	33	210

a) Which year had the highest percentage of students who achieved a grade 7, 8 or 9?

b) What was the highest percentage written as (i) a fraction (ii) as a decimal?

12. A customer had a meal in a restaurant which gave a 25% discount for eating early. The restaurant also puts a 12% service charge on all meals. The waiter made out the bill by first working out the service charge on the cost of the meal and then making the 25% reduction. The customer argued that too much was being charged and the waiter should have reduced the cost of the meal before adding on the service charge. Who was right and why?

13. 3500g is divided in the ratio $5:4:1$

Which of these shows how the 3500g was divided?

(a) 3000g : 400g : 100g

(b) 1750g : 1400g : 350g

(c) 700g : 875g : 1925g

(d) 2250g : 1000g : 350g

14. This table shows the number of entries for Functional Skills assessments in 2018 and 2019.

	Number of entries
January–December 2018	695 465
January–December 2019	582 255

Calculate the percentage decrease in the number of entries from 2018 to 2019.

15. The price of a car is reduced by 40% in a sale to £4800. What was the original price of the car?

14

ESTIMATION AND ROUNDING

[Teachers] should be able to solve mathematical problems using a variety of methods and approaches including: estimating and rounding, sense checking answers, breaking down problems into simpler steps, and explaining and justifying answers using appropriate language.

(DfE, 2020a)

Many of us quite often use estimation: 'I'll be home in about 30 minutes', 'I'll need to get £20 out of the cash machine to pay for a round of drinks'. Estimation usually requires some knowledge of measures: money, weights, lengths, areas, volumes and distances.

Estimating answers to calculations may involve rounding numbers to an acceptable degree of accuracy. For example, suppose that, on a certain day, the population of a small town is exactly 19 279 people. What will the population be two weeks later? It is impossible to say, but we can say that it will be approximately 19 000.

(a) ROUNDING

Sometimes we **round to the nearest 10, 100 or 1000** or some other power of 10. We say that 19 279 equals 19 000 to the nearest thousand. (19 279 is between 19 000 and 20 000 but is nearer to 19 000). We could also say that 19 279 equals 19 300 to the nearest hundred (279 is between 200 and 300 but is nearer to 300.) So 19 279 is rounded down to 19 000 or rounded up to 19 300. This sort of rounding is often used in the media: If you see a headline that says 'Unemployment forecast to be 2 million', then the 2 million is a rounded figure.

A number line can be helpful when rounding numbers:

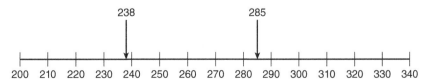

Looking at the number line it is clear that:

- 238 is nearer to 240 than 230, so 238 rounded to the nearest 10 is 240.

- 238 is nearer to 200 than 300, so 238 rounded to the nearest 100 is 200.

- 285 is nearer to 300 than 200, so 285 rounded to the nearest 100 is 300.

- 285 is mid-way between 280 and 290. The convention is that if the last digit is a 5, as here, the number is rounded up so, to the nearest 10, 285 is rounded up to 290, even though it is equidistant from 280 and 290.

This table also shows how to round the numbers 230, 231, 232, 233, ... 239 to the nearest ten.

230	No need to round
231	These are rounded down to 230 as they are nearer to 230 than 240.
232	
233	
234	
235	This is halfway between 230 and 240. The convention is that it rounds up to 240
236	These are rounded up to 240 because they are nearer to 240 than 230.
237	
238	
239	

We can also round decimals to the nearest whole number or to a certain number of decimal places.

Look at this number line:

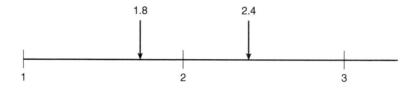

2.4 is nearer to 2 than 3, so 2.4 will round down to 2.

1.8 is nearer to 2 than 1, so 1.8 will round up to 2.

When rounding to the nearest whole number, look at the digit in the first decimal place.

- If it is less than 5, leave the whole number as it is.

- If it is 5 or more, add 1 to the whole number.

Look at this number line:

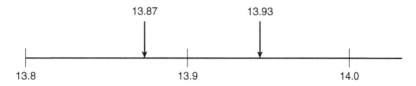

13.87 is nearer to 13.9 than 13.8 so 13.87 is 13.9 to the nearest tenth.

13.93 is nearer to 13.9 than 14.0 so 13.93 is 13.9 to the nearest tenth.

(b) APPROXIMATING

Approximating is about:

- rounding numbers for a calculation so that it is possible to estimate or check the answer mentally. For example, if we want to estimate a 15% discount on £239, we might round the £239 to £240, find 10% = £24, 5% = £12 so the estimate of 15% is £36 [the accurate answer to 15% of £239 is £35.85].

- recognising when an error has been made. For example, the answer to 159 × 159 must be between 100 × 100 and 200 × 200, so between 10000 and 40000. So an answer of 50000 is clearly incorrect.

- working to an appropriate level of detail for the context of the calculation. For example, if we estimate a population to be 62487, we might choose to round the number to 62490 or 62500.

(c) FERMI QUESTIONS

Fermi questions are named after the physicist and Nobel Prize winner, Enrico Fermi. He challenged his students to use estimation, common sense and numerical reasoning to work out quantities that were difficult or impossible to measure. He deliberately posed questions with limited information so that students had to ask more questions or make sensible assumptions. Examples of Fermi questions are:

- How many hairdressers are there in Birmingham?

- How many pennies could fit in a 1 litre jar?

- How long would it take to count to 1 million?

- If everyone in the world moved to England, would they all fit?

By making sensible assumptions, reasonable estimates and using simple calculations, remarkably accurate answers can be reached. You may not need to answer these specific questions, but the same sort of thinking can be applied to check everyday answers and statements. For example, suppose you see a newspaper article that says that 11 million children in the UK receive free school meals. Is this likely to be correct? Well, you probably know that the population of the UK is between 60 and 70 million. Say 65 million. If we make the broad assumption that the number of people of each age is the same, and that people live to 80, then the total number of children of school age (that is, between 5 years old and 18 years old, covering 14 years) will be about ($\frac{14}{80} \times 65$) million. That is, we have an estimate that there are about 11.4 million school children in the UK. In fact, in 2019 there were 10.3 million school children on roll in the UK, so we are not very far out. We can certainly say that there are unlikely to be 11 million children receiving free school meals. (The number in 2019 was just under 2 million.)

Some teachers use Fermi questions with their students to encourage critical thinking and estimation skills to get a 'feel' of whether an answer is reasonable or not. This is what is meant by 'sense checking'. Scientists, economists and engineers regularly use Fermi questions in their work as a way of getting a rough idea of the viability of their plans and projects. It is useful for all of us as teachers and citizens to have these skills.

QUESTIONS

1. Round 1 245 693 to:

    (a) the nearest 10   (b) the nearest 1000   (c) the nearest million

2. Round 3.141 592 6 to:

    (a) 2 decimal places   (b) 4 decimal places   (c) the nearest whole number

3. Estimate the cost of 5 books at £9.99 and 2 books at £15.99

4. Estimate the answer to 15.64 ÷ 4.7

5. A teacher is planning a theatre trip for Year 6.

   - There are 52 students going on the trip.

   - There must be at least one adult for every 10 pupils.

   - Theatre tickets cost £6.45 per person.

   - It costs £98 to hire a 20-seat minibus.

Estimate the total cost.

6. The distance between two train stations is 160 km to the nearest km.

   What is the shortest possible distance between the two stations? What is the furthest apart they could be?

7. A thermometer's digital display is correct to 1 decimal place. The display shows 15.4 °C.

   Which of these temperatures could not be the temperature correct to 3dp?

   15.449 °C   15.380 °C   15.350 °C   15.300 °C   15.406 °C

8. Gopal has an activity tracker. He walked 19 013 metres yesterday.

   (a) Round 19 013 to a sensible degree of accuracy.

   1 mile = 1.6 km

   (b) How many miles did Gopal walk yesterday? Give your answer to the nearest mile.

9. Eli calculates 1234 × 1234 on his calculator and gets the answer 151 782. Explain how Eli should know that he has made a mistake.

10. Bronwen calculates the area of her garden. Which of these is unlikely to be the correct answer?

   (a) 49 m²   (b) 400 m²   (c) 640 000 cm²   (d) 640 000 mm²

11. Estimate the number of primary schools in the UK.

12. Estimate the number of hours of television you will watch in your lifetime.

15

REPRESENTING AND INTERPRETING DATA

Teachers should use data and graphs to interpret information, identify patterns and trends and draw appropriate conclusions. They need to interpret pupil data and understand statistics and graphs in the news, academic reports and relevant papers.

(DfE, 2020a)

Statistics is the practice or science of collecting and analysing numerical data. A statistic (singular) is a number or numerical fact which has been derived from a large set of data.

As a teacher, depending on the Key Stages and subjects you work in, you may have to teach your students to interpret data and statistics. And, as a professional working in education, you will be presented with data and statistics relating to finance, courses, enrolment, attendance, grades, completion, test scores and exam grades, and demographic data. You may also read newspaper articles and research relating to education which present statistics to inform or to make a case. You need to understand how data are collected, represented and interpreted so that you can think critically about the statistics you are presented with. Today, I read in a newspaper that the average salary for a teacher is £38 400. I also read on a website that the median salary for a secondary school teacher in the UK is £29 644 and that 80% of secondary teachers earn between £22 000 and £43 000. Is it possible for both these sources to be correct? Which source tells me the most about what secondary teachers earn?

(a) AVERAGES

The simplest way in which we represent data is by using a single, average, value to represent a whole data set. In everyday language, average is used to mean 'in the middle' or 'normal', as in, 'His exam grades were average'. The mathematical meaning is similar, but the word is used more precisely. There are three averages commonly used.

The **mean** is the average most people give if asked for an average. The mean is found by adding up all the values in a list and dividing this total by the number of values.

The **median** is the middle value when all the values in a list are put in size order. If there is an even number of values in the list there will be two 'middle' values and the median is the mean of these two, in other words halfway between them.

The **mode** is the most common value or category.

For example, for this set of numbers:

3	8	7	2	2	5

- The mean is calculated as $(3 + 8 + 7 + 2 + 2 + 5) \div 6 = 4.5$; notice that the mean does not need to be a whole number.

- The median is found by ordering the numbers 2 2 3 5 7 8 and then calculating $(3 + 5) \div 2 = 4$.

- The mode is 2.

The mode is not often used with numerical data, partly because when all the data values are different there is no mode, and partly because it is quite a simplistic measure of average. It is used with category data, where it is not possible to add up or order the categories. For example, suppose we ask 10 people their ethnicity:

White British	Indian	African	Chinese	Caribbean
African	African	Pakistani	White and Asian	White British

Here the idea of a mean or median ethnic group has no meaning, but the mode would be the largest ethnic group, which in this case would be African.

With numerical data, which of the mean and median averages is better to use? This is not an easy question to answer as it depends what the numbers represent and what we want to use them for. The mean is most commonly used. It is the basis for more advanced statistics and is needed to calculate the standard deviation, which is a measure used to assess how variable a set of data is. It is also needed for many statistical tests. But the median can be more useful when the data are skewed. That is, when we have outliers (values which lie a long way outside most of the data).

For example, suppose we want to compare the test results of two groups of students.

Percentage achieved in test									
Group A	81	85	80	83	84	84	82	80	82	81
Group B	82	82	87	83	83	81	80	81	85	18

Calculating the means and medians for the two groups gives us:

	Median	Mean
Group A	82	82.2
Group B	82	76.2

So, if we use the median as our average, the groups appear to have performed the same. But if we use the mean, Group A appears to have done better. Which do you think is the better average to use?

Group B contains an outlier – the value 18 is quite different from the other scores, which are all in the 80s. This value has 'skewed' the distribution of marks for Group B, resulting in a lower mean. The first thing to do is to check the data. It may be that the 18 should have been 81 but was transcribed incorrectly. If the data are correct, the next thing to do is to check the circumstances surrounding the outlying value. Is that student different from the rest of the group? (For example, did she have to leave the test before the end? Did she miss the teaching for some reason? Is she the only student to have English as an additional language?) There are then two options:

- The first is to leave out the value 18 and recalculate the averages for Group B.

	Median	Mean
Group A	82	82.2
Group B	82	82.7

The median for Group B is unchanged – the outlier did not affect the calculation of the median, as the middle score was still 82. The mean has gone up because the outlying value is no longer depressing the total score for Group B. The groups now appear very similar whichever average we use and we would probably use the mean.

- The second option is to keep all the values but to use the median, which is much less affected by outliers and is more 'robust'.

Generally, the best strategy is to calculate both averages for a set of data. If the mean and median are similar, use the mean for discussion of the data, because almost everybody is familiar with it. If the averages are different, this indicates that the data are skewed and the median is generally more representative.

(b) VARIABILITY

In 2019, 65% of children in Year 6 in England reached the expected standard in reading, writing and maths (www.gov.uk/government/statistics/national-curriculum-assessments-key-stage-2-2019-provisional). This is an average for the whole country. It is actually the median value as well as being the mean value. This is not in itself a very helpful statistic unless you also know where your school/ Local Authority/Trust results are in relation to both the national average and to other similar organisations. It is important to know about the variation in results.

The simplest way of measuring variation is to use the **range**. This is the difference between the maximum value and the minimum value. In 2019, the range for LAs in the percentage of children reaching the expected standard in reading, writing and maths at KS2 was 27 percentage points. (If you simply subtract one percentage from another, use the term 'percentage points' when talking about the difference. This makes it clear that you do not mean a relative change, for example, a 27% change.)

This is still not very useful, but if we also know the minimum and maximum values (53% and 80%) we start to build up an idea of the **distribution** of results by LA:

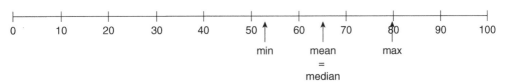

Suppose you worked in an LA, where 70% of children reached the expected standard. You know this is higher than the average, but you might want to know more about the relative position of your LA. The next simplest measure of variation is the interquartile range. To calculate this, we put the data in order, as for the median, and then find the 'median' of the lower half of the data (this is the lower quartile or LQ) and then find the 'median' of the upper half of the data (this is the upper quartile or UQ). So now we have split the data into quarters. For our LA data, the LQ is 62 and the UQ is 68.

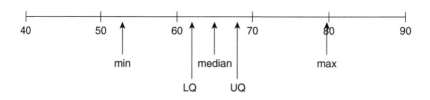

This diagram may be formalised into a 'box plot':

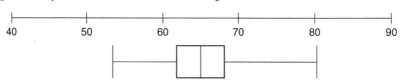

So you now know that the value 70 lies in the top 25% (quarter) of LAs. You also know that the middle half of LAs (the middle 50%) have values between 62 and 68. We call 68 − 62 = 6 the interquartile range (IQR). In this case, the IQR is quite small and half the LAs lie in a narrow band in the middle of the data.

You might now want to know exactly where your LA lies in the top 25%. To work this out, we could split the data into percentiles (or 100ths). In 2019, the value 70 is the 87th percentile, so 13% of LAs had a value greater than 70. Your LA lies in the middle of the top 25% of LAs. This is not obvious without considering the percentiles or the raw data: the diagrams above might lead you to believe that your LA is towards the bottom of the top 25%.

We could also represent the distribution of the data using a **frequency diagram**:

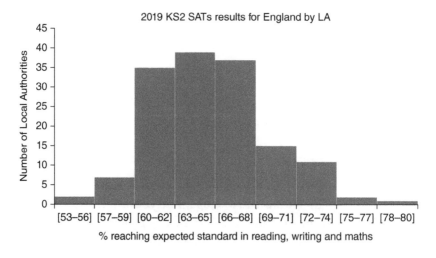

This again shows that a lot of the LAs are grouped closely together in the middle.

Another graph used to represent this type of data is a **cumulative frequency graph**. The cumulative frequency graph for the data above looks like this:

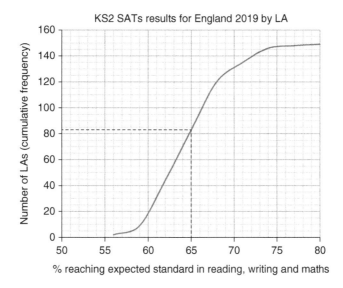

A cumulative frequency graph plots the upper bound of each group (in this case 56, 59, 62, 65, 68, 71, 74, 77 and 80) against the cumulative frequency (here the number of LAs) with value less than or equal to that upper bound. So, for example, we can read from the graph that 83 LAs had a value less than or equal to 65. Notice that the cumulative frequency goes up to 149 because there were 149 LAs. And along the horizontal axis, the curve starts at 56 (not 53) because 56 is the upper bound of the group 53–56.

Unusually, the cumulative frequencies for GCSE grades 9–1 are presented differently as we tend to be more interested in, for example, how many students achieved grade 5 or above, rather than grade 5 or below. (This graph is based on the data from www.gov.uk/government/publications/results-tables-for-gcse-as-and-a-level-results-in-england-2020)

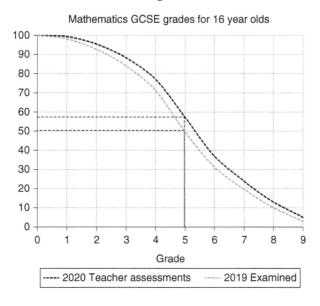

The lines are dotted to indicate that the data are discrete, not continuous: it is not actually possible to get a grade 6.5. 100% of students achieved U or better. In 2019, 50.1% of students achieved a grade 5 or better, while in 2020 this rose to 57.5%. Notice that the graph is decreasing because fewer students achieved 9 (or above) than achieved 5 or above. Usually, cumulative frequency graphs increase. We could reverse the grades on the horizontal axis, but it would also be unusual to have the numbers going down.

(c) TIME SERIES

You might be interested in how something has changed over time. In this case, we could draw a time series graph. The graph below is published by the Office of National Statistics and shows how the number of job vacancies in education has varied over the last 20 years.

Source: https://www.ons.gov.uk/employmentandlabourmarket/peopleinwork/employmentandemployee-types/timeseries/jp9v/lms

The graph clearly shows a sharp decrease in the number of vacancies in 2011 and another in 2020. The fall in 2011 was due to a government drive to cut spending in the public sector. The 2020 fall was due to the coronavirus pandemic.

(d) PIE CHARTS

Pie charts are used to compare proportions. The two pie charts shown here compare the destinations of 16 year olds in 2017/18 on completing year 11. One pie chart represents the destinations of disadvantaged students (defined as those eligible for the Pupil Premium) and the other represents all other students. What would you identify as the main differences between the two groups?

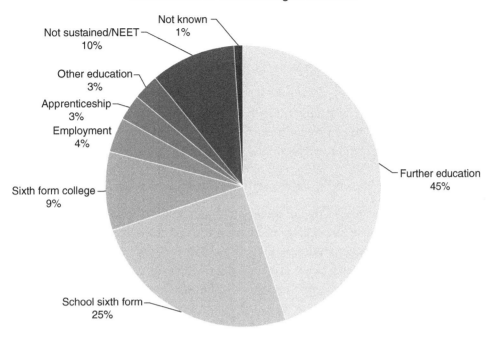

Destinations of disadvantaged students

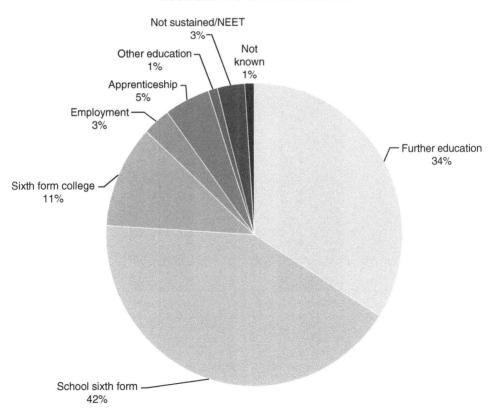

Destinations of all other students

For example, the pie charts show that, in 2017/18

- The most common destination for disadvantaged students was Further Education, while that for other students was a school sixth form.

- 79% of disadvantaged students continued in mainstream education, while 87% of other students did so.

- A higher proportion of disadvantaged students either dropped out of their initial destination in the first few months or did not enter education, training or employment at all (the not sustained/NEET category).

There are also other differences between the two charts which you may have noticed.

The charts do not tell us that a higher *number* of disadvantaged students entered Further Education. This is because in 2017/18, there were 135 755 students eligible for the Pupil Premium and 381 859 other students. 45% of 135 755 is 61 090 and 34% of 381 859 is 129 832. So there were nearly twice as many 'other' students entering FE as there were 'disadvantaged' students. You need to be very careful when interpreting pie charts.

Notice also that there are other ways to display these data than in pie charts. The DfE publication https://assets.publishing.service.gov.uk/government/uploads/system/uploads/attachment_data/file/860135/Destinations_main_text_2020_REV.pdf from which the data were taken actually presents the same data using stacked bar charts.

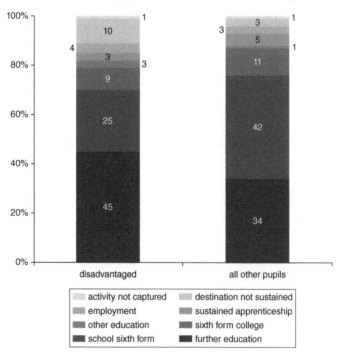

Which presentation do you prefer?

(e) SCATTER DIAGRAMS

Progress 8 (P8) is a secondary accountability measure which aims to measure the progress of students across a selected set of 8 GCSE subjects. Students' results at the end of KS4 are used to create their Attainment 8 (A8) score, which is then compared with the achievement of other students with the same prior attainment. The prior attainment score for a student is the average of their KS2 English and mathematics results. The P8 score is defined as a student's A8 score, minus the average A8 score of all pupils nationally with the same prior attainment at KS2. The individual student P8 scores are averaged to give each school a P8 score.

In 2018, Cambridge Assessment produced these scatter diagrams using Progress 8 data from 2015/16 for mainstream state-funded schools in England.

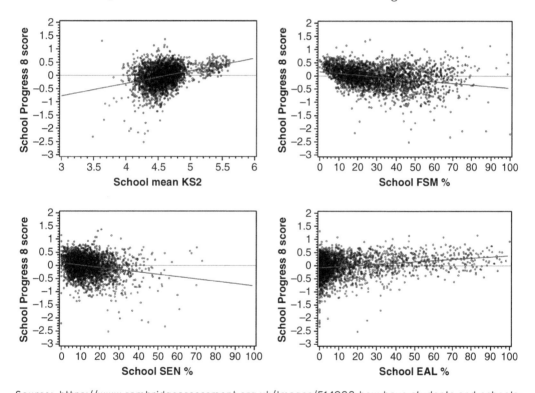

Source: https://www.cambridgeassessment.org.uk/Images/514988-how-have-students-and-schools-performed-on-the-progress-8-performance-measure-.pdf

Each point on a scatter diagram (also called scatter graphs and scatter plots) represents an 'item' that has two measurements associated with it. These measurements are plotted against one another, one along the horizontal axis, the other along the vertical axis. So scatter diagrams show the relationship between two variables. In the Cambridge Assessment diagrams, each point represents a school, and in each diagram, the school's P8 score has been plotted against another variable to show the relationship between P8 scores and

- mean KS2 prior attainment score (mean KS2)

- percentage of students eligible for free school meals (FSM %)

- percentage of students having special educational needs (SEN %)

- percentage of students with English as an additional language (EAL %).

The lines drawn on each diagram are regression lines, also known as lines of best fit. A regression line shows the relationship between the variables. The mean KS2 diagram and the EAL % diagram both show positive correlation. That is, in general, the higher the mean KS2 score (or EAL %), the higher the P8 score. For FSM % and SEN %, the correlation is negative. That is, in general, the higher the FSM % (or SEN %) the lower the P8 score.

The closer the points are to the regression line, the stronger the correlation between the two variables. The strength of correlation can be calculated and given as a number between −1 and +1: you may see these given as R values in research papers. For example, the R value for the mean KS2 data is 0.33, which denotes moderate positive correlation, suggesting that schools with higher prior attaining students also tended to get higher P8 scores on average. For FSM %, the R value was −0.28, suggesting that schools with higher percentages of SEN students tended to have lower P8 scores.

The presence of correlation does not mean that one thing is influencing another, although this could be the case. It just means that the two variables tend to go up and down together. If we plotted students' GCSE grades in maths against their grades in English, the two would be positively correlated. But one grade is not causing the other. Instead, they are both being determined by the same factors. Consider the diagrams above. Do you think they represent causal relationships or are the variables related through other factors? Some questions which could be asked about the diagrams are:

- Given that P8 scores are supposed to take prior attainment into account, why is there still a positive correlation between prior attainment and P8?

- Although FSM % and P8 scores are negatively correlated overall, some schools have high FSM % and high P8 or low FSM % and low P8. Which are these schools and what do they tell us about economic deprivation and achievement?

- Higher SEN % appears associated with lower P8 score. Why do children with statements of SEN make less progress during KS3 and KS4 than other children of the same prior attainment?

- Why do schools with higher EAL % tend to have higher P8 scores?

The answers to these questions are complex and require an analysis of the data behind the scatter diagrams together with an understanding of statistics and the educational context, but you should try to understand why these are good questions to ask.

Graphs and statistics are always just a starting point for discussion and understanding.

QUESTIONS

1. Work out the mean, the median and the mode for this data.

12   5   6   12   10   11   12   6   9   15

2. The pie charts show how Dave spent time on his smartphone and tablet last week.

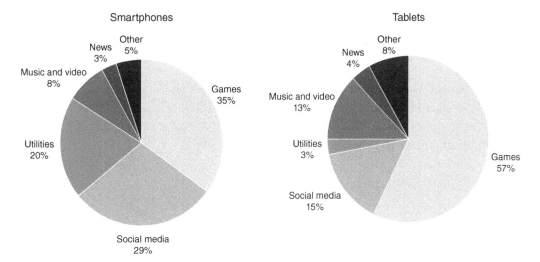

Use the pie charts to say whether each of these statements is true, false or whether you don't have enough information to decide.

a) On both devices, Dave spent longest playing games.

b) Dave uses his tablet more than he uses his phone.

c) Dave played games for longer on his tablet than on his smartphone.

d) Dave spent a higher proportion of time on social media on his smartphone than on his tablet.

e) Dave spent 21% of his total time on the devices playing music and video.

3.

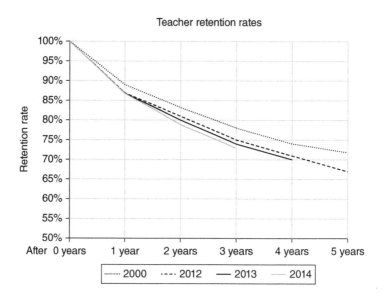

What does this graph tell us?

4. The Income Deprivation Affecting Children Index (IDACI) measures the proportion of all children aged 0 to 15 living in income deprived families. The scatter diagram shows the relationship between IDACI and Progress 8 score for all state-maintained schools in England in 2015/16.

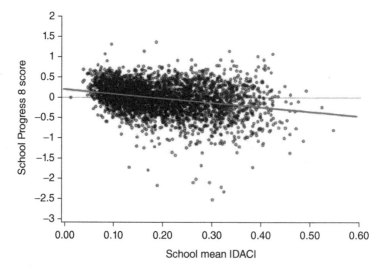

Source: Gill, T. (2018, Sept.)

What does the graph tell us about the relationship between the two measures?

5. You read a report showing this graph.

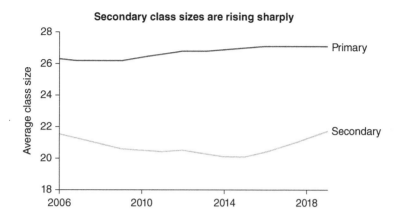

The report says that the average class size in secondary is 'rising sharply'.

Based on the graph, do you think this is true? Explain your answer.

6. This cumulative frequency diagram shows the percentage of 'A' level students who achieved any given grade or better in 2018 and 2019.

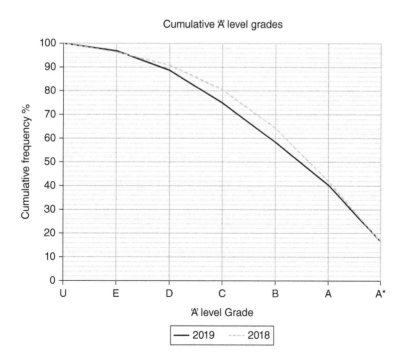

(a) What percentage of the students gained a grade B or better in 2018?

(b) What percentage of students achieved a grade B in 2018?

(c) In which year did the students get higher grades overall? Explain your answer.

7. The prices of a pint of beer in each of 30 pubs in a city in the north of the UK and 30 in the south of the UK were recorded and the following box plots produced to show the two distributions:

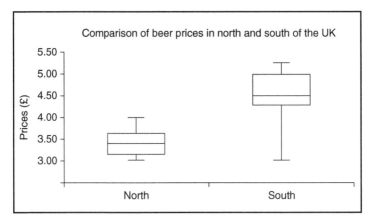

Look carefully at the diagram and say whether each of the following statements is true or false:

(a) The lowest price is to be found in the north.

(b) The interquartile range for the north is larger.

(c) The range of prices in the south is larger.

(d) The median price in the south is about £4.50.

(e) The highest price in the north would be in the lowest 25% of prices in the south.

(f) The middle 50% of prices in the south is symmetrically distributed.

8. The crowd sizes for 22 home league games played by The Reds were

1976	2162	1502	1782	1523	2033	1564	1320	1951
1714	1841	1648	1345	1837	1718	2047	1954	2000
1479	2571	1739	1781					

The crowd sizes for the 22 home games played by a rival club, The Blues, were

1508	2055	2085	2098	1745	1939	2116	1956	2075
1702	1995	2391	1964	1879	1813	2144	1958	2203
2149	2064	1777	1989					

Find the median, quartiles and interquartile range for each team. Construct two boxplots and use your results to compare the crowd sizes for the two teams.

9. The mean age of the 11 members of a football team is 22 years.

When one member of the football team is sent off, the mean age of the rest of the team is 21 years.

(a) How old was the player who was sent off?

The modal age of the 11 players is 17.

Only the three youngest players are aged 17.

The median age of the 11 players is 20.

(b) What is the maximum possible age of one of the players?

The football club does a survey and finds that the mean age of its supporters is 25 and the median age is 20.

(c) Which of the following graphs could show the age distribution of the club's supporters?

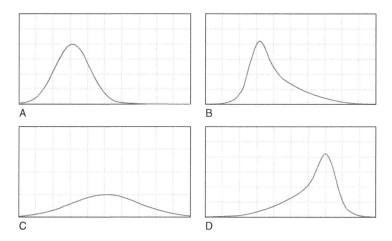

A   B

C   D

10. I found some old matchboxes in my cupboard and counted the numbers of matches in each. The median, mode and mean of these counts were 3, 4 and 5, respectively. How many boxes did I find and how many matches were in each? What is the smallest number of matchboxes I could have found?

16

PROBLEM SOLVING

Teachers ... should be able to solve mathematical problems using a variety of methods and approaches including: estimating and rounding, sense checking answers, breaking down problems.

(DfE, 2020a)

There are two sorts of 'mathematical problems': those that arise in real life and puzzles that are constructed to make you think mathematically.

In real life, maths questions arise in context and not as disembodied calculations which are clearly stated. For example, it is straightforward to calculate $93.2 \div 10$ or 93.2×10 with or without a calculator. But it is unlikely that anyone will ever ask you to do that for them. Now suppose a hat costs 93.2 Yuan, £1 = 10.00 Yuan, and you want to know how much the hat costs in pounds. Here you have to decide what calculation to do, and that is what makes it a mathematical problem.

Mathematical 'puzzles' do not arise naturally but are constructed to encourage students and others to develop wider problem-solving skills, such as logical thinking, the ability to structure a problem, the ability to explain and mathematical 'resilience'. Some people enjoy doing this type of problem solving for fun, but even if you do not, the skills you use to solve these types of problem will be useful to you as a teacher and more generally as a citizen.

Real-life problems and mathematical puzzles, unlike specific calculations in mathematics, do not come with a set of rules that, when applied, lead to the answer. It is therefore difficult to follow the pattern of the previous chapters where rules, methods and procedures are explained and supported with worked examples. However, the following points are good general advice.

- Make a note of the key information you have. Perhaps draw a diagram.

- Make sure you are clear about what you want to find out.

- There may be more than one approach to getting a correct answer.

- Trial and improvement is sometimes a good way to start with puzzles.

- Check your answer using estimation or by considering whether it makes sense.

(a) REAL-LIFE PROBLEM SOLVING

Here are three examples:

1. In 2018, there were 1205 children on your school roll. In 2019 there were 1320. The head teacher says that the school roll has increased by nearly 10% between 2018 and 2019. You want to check whether she is correct. How could you do this?

2. The table below shows part of the 2019 population of the UK split into different age groups.

Age (years)	0-4	5-9	10-14	15-19	20-24	25-29	30-34	35-39
Population (million)	3.86	4.15	3.95	3.66	4.15	4.51	4.5	4.4

Estimate the number of children in years 7 to 11 and the number of teachers required to teach them.

3. School A has 800 pupils and a pupil : teacher ratio of 20 : 1.

School B has 1200 pupils and a pupil : teacher ratio of 16 : 1.

The two schools merge to form a new school.

If all the pupils and teachers transfer to the new school, what will its pupil : teacher ratio be?

Have a go at these three problems before you read on.

POSSIBLE SOLUTIONS

1. This is relatively straightforward, but you have a choice of mathematical methods:

You could increase 1205 by 10% (1325.5) and compare it with 1320. 1320 is quite close to 1325 so she is right. To increase 1205 by 10% you can either find 10% and add it on, or you can multiply 1205 by 1.10.

Or you could calculate the percentage increase exactly (9.54%), which is nearly 10%, so again she is right. To calculate the % increase, you could either calculate 1320 − 1205 = 115 and then calculate 115 out of 1205 as a percentage.

Or you can calculate $1320 \div 1205 = 1.0954$ and recognise that this multiplier represents a 9.54% increase.

2. The first step is to estimate the number of children in years 7 to 11. In the 10–19 age range there are $3.95 + 3.66 = 7.61$ million students. Averaging this over the 10 years in the period 10–19 gives $7.61 \div 10 = 0.761$ million, or 761 000 children per year. So the number of students in the five years from year 7 to 11 will be about 0.761×5, which gives us an estimate of about 3.805 million children.

    You now need to estimate the number of teachers. If every child is in a class at the same time, the smallest number of teachers required would be 3.805 million ÷ mean class size, giving one teacher for every class. If we assume the mean class size to be 25, then we need $3\,805\,000 \div 25 = 152\,200$ teachers. Of course, there are more teachers than this because of PPA and cover and other responsibilities. We could increase 152 200 by 20% to allow for this, increasing our estimate to 182 640 FTE teachers. This is still likely to be an underestimate because independent schools and special schools have smaller teacher : student ratios and because some teachers do not teach a full timetable of KS3 and KS4 because of other responsibilities. In fact, the average class size in mainstream secondary schools is about 22, which would give us an estimate of 207 545 FTE teachers. (The calculation is $3\,805\,000 \div 22 = 172\,955$ then increase this figure by 20%.)

3. School A has $800 \div 20 = 40$ teachers.

    School B has $1200 \div 16 = 75$ teachers.

    So the new school has $800 + 1200 = 2000$ pupils and $40 + 75 = 115$ teachers.

    Its pupil : teacher ratio is 2000 : 115 which would be simplified to 17.4 : 1 (In maths we usually write ratios using whole numbers, but in real-life contexts, they are often in the form $1 : n$ or $n : 1$ where n is a decimal number.)

(b) MATHEMATICAL 'PUZZLE' PROBLEM SOLVING

Here are two examples:

1. The same number is added to both numerator and denominator of the fraction $\dfrac{5}{11}$.

    The resulting fraction is equal to $\dfrac{2}{3}$.

    What is the number?

2. Adam paid £30 for four presents.

    A   B   C   D

For A and B he paid £17 in total.

For B and C he paid £15 in total.

For C and D he paid £13 in total.

For A and C he paid £18 in total.

How much did Adam pay for each present?

Have a go at both these problems before reading on.

POSSIBLE SOLUTIONS

1. There are (at least) three approaches to this problem. You might have tried adding ones to the numerator and denominator until you got to a fraction that was equal to $\frac{2}{3}$.

$$\frac{5}{11} \rightarrow \frac{6}{12} \rightarrow \frac{7}{13} \rightarrow \frac{8}{14} \rightarrow \frac{9}{15} \rightarrow \frac{10}{16} \rightarrow \frac{11}{17} \rightarrow \frac{12}{18}$$
$$\qquad\quad \frac{1}{2} \qquad\qquad\quad \frac{4}{7} \quad \frac{3}{5} \quad \frac{5}{8} \qquad\qquad \frac{2}{3}$$

You added 7 ones on, so the answer is 7.

Or you might have started with $\frac{2}{3}$ and listed equivalent fractions:

The list of equivalent fractions is:

$$\frac{2}{3} \rightarrow \frac{4}{6} \rightarrow \frac{6}{9} \rightarrow \frac{8}{12} \rightarrow \frac{10}{15} \rightarrow \frac{12}{18} \rightarrow \frac{14}{21} \rightarrow \dots$$

The first fraction in this list we need to consider, where the numerator is greater than 5 and the denominator is greater than 11, is $\frac{8}{12} = \frac{5+3}{11+1}$ the next fraction is $\frac{10}{15} = \frac{5+5}{11+4}$ and then $\frac{12}{18} = \frac{5+7}{11+7}$. Here, the same number has been added to both the numerator and the denominator. So the answer is 7,

Or you could have used an algebraic approach:

$$\frac{5+n}{11+n} = \frac{2}{3}$$

So $15 + 3n = 22 + 2n$

which solves to give $n = 7$

2. There are also alternative approaches here.

    You might solve this by trying different numbers.

    $A + B = 17$ so we could try $A = 8$ and $B = 9$. That would make $C = 6$ and $D = 7$. But then $A + C = 14$ not 18.

    We could try $A = 9$ and $B = 8$. Then $C = 7$ and $D = 6$. But this gives us $A + C = 16$ not 18.

    What if we try $A = 10$ and $B = 7$? Then $C = 8$ and $D = 5$. This makes all the sums correct and the values $(10 + 7 + 8 + 5)$ total 30 so this is a solution to the problem.

    Or you might have written something like

    $A + B = 17$............①

    $B + C = 15$............②

    $C + D = 13$............③

    $A + C = 18$............④

    Subtracting the 2nd equation from the 1st gives $A - C = 2$

    So, A is 2 more than C i.e. $A = C + 2$

    Subtracting the 3rd equation from the 2nd gives $B - D = 2$

    So, B is 2 more than D   i.e. $B = D + 2$

    Subtracting the 3rd equation from the 4th gives $A - D = 5$

    So, A is 5 more than D   i.e. $A = D + 5$

    Then we can try a value for D, say 6, making $A = 11$, $B = 8$ and $C = 9$ but these add up to 34. If we try $D = 5$, then $A = 10$, $B = 7$ and $C = 8$. These values $(10 + 7 + 8 + 5)$ do add to 30 and so this is a solution to the problem.

    Or you might take a purely algebraic approach:

    $A + B + B + C = 17 + 15 = 32$

    So $A + C + 2B = 32$

    But $A + C = 18$ so $18 + 2B = 32$

    $B = 7$

    When $B = 7$, $A = 10$, $C = 8$ and $D = 5$ so these are the values we want.

Whichever way you approached all these problems, the crucial skill was to understand and structure the problem in a way that allowed you either to be systematic, or to use an algebraic method. In either case, you were thinking logically and problem solving.

QUESTIONS

1. A teacher is taking a group of children to Forest School by minibus. The site is 8 miles away. How many minutes will the journey take if they travel at an average speed of 25 mph?

2. A teacher is planning to read a story to his Year 6 class. He will read for 15 minutes at the end of each day. The book has 144 pages and about 170 words on each page. The teacher reads at a speed of 160 words a minute. How many weeks will it take him to finish reading the book to his class?

3. A course is to be delivered in two-hour sessions on Wednesdays and Fridays. The tutor has been allocated 40 hours of contact time. The course will begin on Wednesday 16 September. The college is closed for the week beginning 26 October. On what date will the course finish?

4. A school is organising a visit to Berlin. A German hotel offers accommodation at €135 per person for a three-night stay. The exchange rate is £1 = €1.463 and the bank charges a 5% transaction fee. What is the total cost in pounds of paying for accommodation for 40 people for a three-night stay?

5. An independent school is given a large donation. The school invests the money for 10 years at a compound interest rate of 2%. What is this investment worth at the end of the 10 years as a percentage of the original investment?

6. A group of students is producing a school newsletter. They plan to print 800 copies. There will be eight pages in each newsletter. 25% of the space will be filled with photos and there will be an average of 320 words per page. Students already have seven articles which have these word counts:

Sports update	285 words
Letters	340 words
About the editorial team	28 words
Bullying survey	185 words
Revue of recent drama	289 words
School news update	456 words
Comment	286 words

   About how many pages are left to fill?

7. A teacher is making a fruit cocktail for a school fair.

   She has found two recipes:

Recipe A	Recipe B
2 measures of cranberry juice	3 measures of cranberry juice
3 measures of orange juice	4 measures of orange juice
4 measures of sparkling water	5 measures of sparkling water

   She chooses the recipe with the highest proportion of fruit juice.

   She estimates that she will need 250 cups holding 200 ml.

   - A pack of 50 cups costs £1
   - A 1 litre carton of juice costs £1.25
   - A pack of 6 × 1 litre bottles of sparkling water costs £2.25
   - A 1.5 litre pack of sparkling water costs £0.85

   She would like to make about 5p profit on each cup of fruit drink.

   How much should she charge for each cup of fruit drink?

8. A food technology teacher is planning a demonstration.

   These are the tasks he has to do, but they are not in order.

Job A **Heat and stir the sauce** Takes 3 minutes Must be completed just before the fish is served	**Job B** **Make the sauce** Takes 7 minutes Must be done before heating the sauce

Job C **Prepare the vegetables** Takes 4 minutes Must be done before making the sauce and before cooking the vegetables	**Job D** **Skin and bone the fish** Takes 5 minutes Must be done before cooking the fish

Job E **Cook the vegetables** Takes 10 minutes Must be completed just before the fish is served	**Job F** **Serve up the meal** Takes 2 minutes

Job G
Cook the fish
Takes 10 minutes

The fish can be left to cook in the oven and the vegetables can be left cooking on the hob while he does something else.

If the demonstration starts at 1.05 pm, what is the earliest time it could finish?

9. Comment critically on each of these (made up) newspaper headlines:

   (a) **Eating sweets better than reading!** Schools told to sell sweets as study shows that the number of dental cavities in children is positively correlated with the size of their vocabulary. The same study also found that children with bigger feet spell better.

   (b) **Diet drinks cause obesity!** A study by leading health experts has found that the more diet drinks people drink, the fatter they are. Schools have been advised to sell more sugary drinks to reduce obesity in children.

   (c) **Antibiotics scare!** The safety of antibiotics is being questioned as the use of medication in children is shown to be associated with the subsequent development of asthma.

10. You have applied for a job in a school which has five classes in Year 7. At interview, the head tells you that the average class size in Year 7 is 24 pupils. You take the job and when you start the union rep tells you that the average class size in Year 7 is 34 pupils. Is it necessarily true that either the head or the union rep is wrong? Explain your answer.

11. A square piece of paper is folded in half. The resulting rectangle has a perimeter of 12 cm.

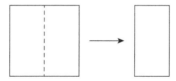

    What was the area of the original square?

12. Each shape stands for a number.

    The numbers shown are the totals of the line of four numbers in a row or a column.

◇	✳	◇	θ	
✳	θ	✳	◇	43
θ	θ	θ	θ	36
◇	✳	✳	◇	
			38	

Find the remaining totals.

13. Each shape inside the large square is also a square. The number inside each square gives the length of its sides, in cm.

What are the values of A, B, C, and D?

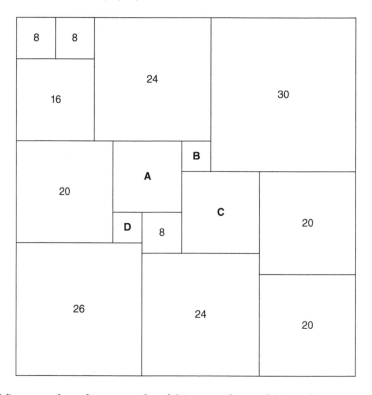

14. A set of five numbers has a mode of 24, a median of 21 and a mean of 20.

What could the numbers be?

15. Hayley put some 20p coins on the table.

Half of them were 'heads up'.

Hayley turned over two of the coins and then one-third of them were 'heads up'.

How many coins did Hayley put on the table?

16. (a) Sally has two discs, one white and one black.

The white disc has ④ on one side and ⑤ on the other.

The black disc has ❷ on one side and ❽ on the other.

If Sally throws the discs in the air they could land like this: ④ ❷ giving a total score of 6, or they could land like this: ⑤ ❽ giving a total score of 13.

What other ways could they land and what would the total score be in each case?

(b) Bob has two discs like Sally's but they have different numbers.

The white disc has ③ on one side and ⑥ on the other.

The black disc has ❼ on one side and ❿ on the other.

Write down all the possible ways that Bob's discs could land and give the total score in each case.

(c) Nicola has two discs of different colours. Each disc has a number on each side. When Nicola's discs land, the different possible total scores are 4, 6, 10, 13.

What numbers are on Nicola's discs?

(d) Ian has two discs of different colours. Each disc has a number on each side. When Ian's discs land, the only possible total scores are 3, 7, 11.

What numbers are on Ian's discs?

17

ANSWERS

CHAPTER 10: INITIAL AUDIT

1. (a) ÷100   (b) ×100 000   (c) ÷1000   (d) ×100   (e) ×1000   (f) ÷100

2. Eight teams with 7 boys in each team gives 56 boys. There are 96 children in total so there must be 40 girls, which gives 5 girls in each team. Or 96 ÷ 8 = 12 so there are 12 children per team. There are 7 boys in a team so there will be 5 girls.

3. Finding the lowest common denominator, which is 8, the addition becomes

   $\dfrac{6}{8} + \dfrac{1}{8} = \dfrac{7}{8}$

   (It is also possible to use a denominator of 16 or 32, giving $\dfrac{24}{32} + \dfrac{4}{32} = \dfrac{28}{32} = \dfrac{7}{8}$ or

   $\dfrac{12}{16} + \dfrac{2}{16} = \dfrac{14}{16} = \dfrac{7}{8}$.)

4. The ratio is 15 : 4 : 1, so the total number of parts is 15 + 4 + 1 = 20.

   So, 20 parts weigh 4 g and thus 1 part weighs 4 ÷ 20 = $\dfrac{1}{5}$ g.

   Therefore, 15 parts weigh $15 \times \dfrac{1}{5}$ = 3 g (Check: the answer must be less than 4 g – the weight of the ring.)

5. Finding a number 'mid-way' between two other numbers is effectively the same as finding the mean. So add the two fractions and then divide by 2.

   $3\dfrac{3}{4} + \dfrac{3}{4} = \dfrac{15}{4} + \dfrac{3}{4} = \dfrac{18}{4} = 4\dfrac{1}{2}$. Dividing $4\dfrac{1}{2}$ by 2 gives $2\dfrac{1}{4}$ i.e. $\dfrac{9}{2} \times \dfrac{1}{2} = \dfrac{9}{4} = 2\dfrac{1}{4}$

   or dividing $\dfrac{18}{4}$ by 2 gives $\dfrac{9}{4} = 2\dfrac{1}{4}$

6. The ratio is 3 : 1 that is 3 parts of oil to 1 part of vinegar.

   (a) 72 ml of oil represents 3 parts so 1 part is 72 ÷ 3 = 24. So, 24 ml of vinegar is needed. (Check: answer must be less than 72 ml.)

(b) there are 3 + 1 i.e. 4 parts, so 4 parts represents 1 litre. 1 part represents 250 ml so the chef needs 250 ml of vinegar and 750 ml of oil. (Check: volume of oil must be greater than the volume of vinegar.)

7. (a) 75% of 400 = 0. 75 × 400 = 300 people

(b) $\dfrac{7}{10}$ of 400 = $\dfrac{7}{10}$ × 400 = 7 × 40 = 280 people

(c) 120 as a percentage of 400 is $\dfrac{120}{400} \times 100\% = 30\%$

8. (a) Zoo costs are 76 × £8 + 30 × £4 = £728,

(b) Museum costs are 60 × £8 + 30 × £6 = £660,

(c) Space science show costs are 40 × £8 + 30 × £12 = £680,

The difference between the least and most expensive trips is £728 – £660 = £68,

(Remember to double the distances: the pupils will return to school.)

9. For example, you can check by rounding both numbers. 5239 rounded to the nearest 1000 gives 5000. 142 378 rounded to the nearest 100 000 gives 100 000. 100 000 × 5000 = 500 000 000 so the correct answer must be bigger than that, and 74 587 642 is smaller.

10. There are two approaches. One is to use a calculator to do the divisions and compare the sizes of the decimal answers:

$\dfrac{11}{16} = 0.6875$ $\dfrac{1}{2} = 0.5$ $\dfrac{5}{8} = 0.625$ $\dfrac{15}{16} = 0.9375$ $\dfrac{3}{4} = 0.75$

The other is to find a common denominator. The lowest is 16, and the fractions then become:

$\dfrac{11}{16}$ $\dfrac{8}{16}$ $\dfrac{10}{16}$ $\dfrac{15}{16}$ $\dfrac{12}{16}$

It is straightforward now to put them in size order by looking at the size of the numerators, giving $\dfrac{8}{16}$ $\dfrac{10}{16}$ $\dfrac{11}{16}$ $\dfrac{12}{16}$ $\dfrac{15}{16}$

Changing these fractions to the form they were given at the start then the order is:

$\dfrac{1}{2}$ $\dfrac{5}{8}$ $\dfrac{11}{16}$ $\dfrac{3}{4}$ $\dfrac{15}{16}$

11. A loss of 16% means that Sarah's guitar is now worth 84% of the original price.

So 1% of the original price is = £54.39 ÷ 84 = £0.6475 and 100% of original price is £0.6475 × 100 = £64.75. (Understanding the first line of this answer is of key importance.)

Alternatively:

Let the original price be £P.

84% of P, i.e. $0.84 \times P = £54.39$ so $P = \dfrac{54.39}{0.84}$

Hence P = £64.75

12. (a) $210 \times £13.80 + 90 \times £8.50 = £3663$

(b) $\dfrac{120}{200} = 60\%$

(c) Cost = £9787 Total income = £13 645

Profit = £13 645 – £9787 = £3858

$\dfrac{3858}{9787}$ is approximately $\dfrac{4000}{10000}$ or $\dfrac{4}{10}$ or $\dfrac{2}{5}$. (Note the fraction is the cash profit divided by the original cost, not divided by the income.)

13. (a) 23.46   (b) 23 459 000   (c) 4.79 m

14. (a) The range is the highest mark minus the lowest mark.

For class 10A the range is 75% – 15% = 60%

For class 10B the range is 92% – 20% = 72%

For class 10C the range is 87% – 30% = 57%

For class 10D the range is 90% – 30% = 60%

So, class 10B has the greatest range.

(b) The median is represented by the line across the middle of the box.

For class 10A the median is 35%, the lowest mark is 15%, the difference = 20%.

For class 10B the median is 50%, the lowest mark is 20%, the difference = 30%.

For class 10C the median is 55%, the lowest mark is 30%, the difference = 25%.

For class 10D the median is 65%, the lowest mark is 30%, the difference = 35%.

So, class 10D has a median mark 35 marks above the lowest mark.

(c) The interquartile range for class 10A is 55% minus 25%, which is 30%.

15. (a) The median time is the time spent by 50% of the students, so it is 8 hours.

(b) 6 hours' work was done by 75% of the students. 75% of 240 = 180

16. (a) As the straight line on the graph shows equal scores on both tests, the students who gained the same mark in both tests will be shown by points on the line. There are 6 students.

(b) If it helps, draw a straight line across the graph starting at 80% on the vertical axis. There are 7 students who either lie on this line or are above the line.

17. $\frac{1}{4}$ of 28 is 7 games. $\frac{1}{3}$ of 18 is 6 games. So the Under 13s won more games.

(Note: when comparing two pie charts you will need to consider if they represent different amounts, as in this question. If they do then you should not compare the sizes of the different sectors.)

18. Mean: $(3.6 + 3.5 + 3.2 + 3.2 + 3.4 + 3.9 + 3.1 + 3.2 + 3.5 + 3.8) \div 10$

= 34.4 ÷ 10 = 3.44

Mode = 3.2, the most frequent number

Median: 3.1   3.2   3.2   3.2   3.4   3.5   3.5   3.6   3.8   3.9

$(3.4 + 3.5) \div 2 = 3.45$

(Note: remember, to find the median you must put the numbers in size order. In this question there are an even number of numbers so the median is the mean of the middle two numbers.)

19. LA 1: mean 0.164   median 0.25

LA 2: mean −0.044   median 0.2

It is probably better to use the median because the outlying value of −1.2 is causing the mean for LA 2 to be very low. In reality, one would also need to check which school the −1.2 represented, and if the score was correct, why it was so low.

20. World population is 7.8 billion. You need to estimate how many people have a mobile phone (in fact, it is about 5 billion – were you close?). Then say one-third of these are asleep at any point. So about 3.3 billion are awake with a phone. How many of your (16) waking hours do you spend on your phone? Are you typical? Research suggests that people use their mobile phones for an average of 3 hours 15 minutes a day, with 20% of people using it for more than 4 hours 30 minutes a day. But let's say 3.25 hours a day. $(3.25 \div 16) \times 3.3$ billion gives us about 0.67 billion, or 670 million people. That's twice the population of the USA.

21. You could try some numbers: $\frac{11}{16} = 0.69$, $\frac{12}{17} = 0.71$, $\frac{13}{18} = 0.72$. etc. until you get to

$\frac{20}{25} = 0.8 = 80\%$, so 25 questions in total.

Or you could say he gets 5 wrong. 5 represents 20% so 100% is 5 × 5 = 25 questions.

Or you could take an algebraic approach, with x being the number of additional questions: $\dfrac{10+x}{15+x} = 0.8$ so $10+x = 0.8(15+x)$ thus $10 + x = 12 + 0.8x$ and $0.2x = 2$. Then $x = 10$ and $15 + x$ gives us 25 questions.

22. For the house where he made a loss, $252\ 000 = 0.8 \times$ cost, so the cost = 315 000.

For the house where he made a profit, $252\ 000 = 1.2 \times$ cost, so the cost = 210 000.

Total cost = £525 000. Total selling price = £504 000, giving a loss of £21 000.

23. (a) The mean of the current numeracy marks = $256 \div 4 = 64$.

The mean of the literacy marks = $315 \div 5 = 63$.

So, there is 1 mark difference.

(b) To gain a mean score of 68 the total of the 5 marks will be $5 \times 68 = 340$.

The total of the current 4 marks = 256.

So, she needs to score $340 - 256 = 84$ marks.

24. $\dfrac{12 \times 40}{20} + \dfrac{24 \times 60}{40} = 24 + 36 = 60$

CHAPTER 12: CALCULATING WITH WHOLE NUMBERS

1. (a) 3388   (b) 424   (c) 48 120   (d) 31   (e) 143

2. $18 \times 36 \times 14 = 9072$

3. (a) $366 \div 12 = 30.5$ so 31 adults, $366 + 31 = 397$ people

   (b) $397 \div 53 = 7.49$, so 8 coaches (remember to round up in situations like this. If you rounded down to 7 only 7×53 or 371 people could travel, meaning that 26 people would not be able to go).

4. $104\ 301 - 103\ 827 = 474$

5. $50 \div 500 = 0.1$ mm

6. The number of gallons used is $200 \div 32 = 6.25$

   The number of litres is $6.25 \times 4.546 = 28.4125$

   The cost is $28.4125 \times 1.19 = 33.81$, which rounds to £34 to the nearest £.

7. (a) $(37 \times 21) + 223 = 1000$ (b) $27 + (36 \times 18) = 675$

   (c) $476 - (2040 \div 24) = 391$ (d) $(720 - 340) \times 42 \div 20 = 798$

8. The route is $5 \times 4 \rightarrow 20 - 4 \rightarrow 16 \times 6 \rightarrow = 96 + 4 \rightarrow 100$

With questions or challenges like this, it sometimes is helpful to work backwards, reversing the operations so that, for example, + becomes – and × becomes ÷ .

We want the answer to be 100, so start with 100. The options are (a) to subtract 4, giving 96 or (b) multiply by 3 giving 300. 300 seems a large number to deal with so look at 96. The options are now to divide 96 by 4, giving 24, or divide 96 by 6, giving 16. Then $16 + 4 = 20$ $20 \div 4 = 5$ $5 - 5 = 0$.

9. (a) In 2015/16, the total was 4 615 172 + 3 193 418, giving 7 808 590

In 2019/20 the total is 4 714 722 + 3 409 277, giving a total of 8 123 999

The difference is 315 409 students.

(b) In 2019/20, the average is $\dfrac{3409\,277}{3456} = 986(.48)$

In 2015/16, the average was $\dfrac{3193\,418}{3401} = 938(.96)$ so 2019/20 is higher.

10. Total from papers 1 and 2 is 140. Minimum mark is 260 so she needs to gain 120 marks on paper 3.

11. (a) £388 million × 52 gives £20 176 million or £20 176 000 000

(b) £388 million ÷ 7 = £55.428 571 million or £55 428 571

12. Weighted score = $\dfrac{420}{100} + \dfrac{900}{100} + 12 = 42 + 9 + 12 = 63$

CHAPTER 13: FRACTIONS, DECIMALS, PERCENTAGES (INCLUDING RATIO AND PROPORTION)

1   (a) $0.4 = \dfrac{4}{10} = \dfrac{2}{5}$,   40%   (b) 0.7,   70%   (c) $\dfrac{36}{100} = \dfrac{9}{25}$,   0.36

(d) $\dfrac{59}{100}$,   59%   (e) 0.27,   27%   (f) $\dfrac{17}{100}$,   0.17

2.   (a) £9   (b) 156   (c) 187.5 cm   (d) 88   (e) 25.6   (f) 93.6

3.   Cannot have a decimal in the numerator, so in (a) can't have $\dfrac{2.5}{5}$ or in (b) $\dfrac{9.5}{30}$

So there must be a difference in the numerators that is greater than 1.

(a) Using the lowest common denominator: $\dfrac{2}{5} = \dfrac{4}{10}$ and $\dfrac{3}{5} = \dfrac{6}{10}$ so between these two fractions is $\dfrac{5}{10} = \dfrac{1}{2}$

Or, using 20 as the common denominator:

$\dfrac{2}{5} = \dfrac{8}{20}$ and $\dfrac{3}{5} = \dfrac{12}{20}$ so halfway between these fractions lies $\dfrac{10}{20}$.

(b) $\dfrac{3}{10} = \dfrac{9}{30}$, $\dfrac{1}{3} = \dfrac{10}{30}$. Change into fractions with denominator of 60, giving

$\dfrac{18}{60}$ and $\dfrac{20}{60}$ so a fraction that lies halfway between $\dfrac{3}{10}$ and $\dfrac{1}{3}$ is $\dfrac{19}{60}$.

4. English is $\dfrac{98}{123}$ giving 79.7%; History is $\dfrac{123}{157}$ giving 78.3%

Psychology is $\dfrac{105}{132}$ giving 79.5%

5. (a) $\dfrac{2}{3} \times 450 + \dfrac{1}{2} \times 300 = 450$ (b) $\dfrac{450}{750} = \dfrac{3}{5}$

6. The 20% discount offer: £9.50 × 0.8 = £7.60 (Remember that 20% taken off leaves 80%. So, multiply by 0.8 or find 20% of £9.50 and subtract this number from £9.50)

7. 3.1, 3.29, 3.47, 3.53, 3.8 or 3.1, 3.29, 3.47, $3\dfrac{53}{100}$, $3\dfrac{8}{10}$

8. $\dfrac{5}{23.5} = 21.27\%$ so 21%

9. (a) 69 students went swimming so the girls were $\dfrac{27}{69} = 39.1\%$ of that total.

    (b) There are 60 girls in total so the percentage who chose tennis = $\dfrac{33}{60} = 55\%$.

    (c) The total number of students = 130   69 chose swimming. $\dfrac{69}{130} = 53\%$

10. (a) 28 000 ÷ 7 = 4000. So one club will receive 6 × 4000 = 24 000 tickets.

    The other club will receive 4000 tickets.

    (b) 21 600 represents 6 parts, so 1 part is 3600, which is the allocation for the away team.

    (c) 2500 tickets represents 1 part, so the opponents receive 6 × 2500 = 15 000 tickets.

11. (a) In 2017 the total number of students gaining grades 7, 8 or 9 = 24

    $\dfrac{24}{209} = 11.48\%$

In 2018, the total number of students gaining grades 7, 8 or 9 = 35

$$\frac{35}{188} = 18.6\%$$

In 2019, the total number of students gaining grades 7, 8 or 9 = 42

$$\frac{42}{210} = 20\%$$

2019 had the highest percentage achieving grades 7, 8 or 9

(b) (i) As a fraction 20% = $\frac{1}{5}$ (ii) As a decimal 20% = 0.2

12. It makes no difference. If the cost of the meal were £C then the waiter's method is C × 1.12 × 0.75. The customer's method is C × 0.75 × 1.12 (The order in which you multiply numbers together doesn't matter: e.g. $2 \times 3 \times 4 = 3 \times 4 \times 2 = 4 \times 2 \times 3$)

13. 5 + 4 + 1 = 10,   3500 ÷ 10 = 350 which is 1 part.

Then 5 parts is 5 × 350 = 1750 and 4 parts is 1400. So (b) is correct.

14. The difference is 113 210. So the % difference is

$$\frac{113210}{695465} \times 100 = 16.3\%$$

15. 4800 = 60% of the original price. So 1% of the original price is 4800 ÷ 60 = £80. Then 100% of the original price is 80 × 100 = £8000 (look back at the notes on reverse percentages).

CHAPTER 14: ESTIMATION AND ROUNDING

1. 1 245 693 rounds to:

   (a) 1 245 690 as 93 is nearer 90 than 100

   (b) 1 246 000 as 5693 is nearer 6000 than 7000

   (c) 1 000 000 as 1 245 693 is nearer 1 000 000 than 2 000 000

2. 3.141 592 6 rounds to:

   (a) 3.14 because 3.141 is nearer 3.14(0) than 3.142

   (b) 3.1416 because 3.141 59 is nearer to 3.1416 than 3.1415

   (c) 3 because 3.1 is nearer 3 than 4

3. Round each of the costs to the nearest whole number so the estimate will be:

   $5 \times £10 + 2 \times £16 = £82$

4. Round 15.64 up to 16 and 4.7 up to 5, giving $16 \div 5 = 3.2$

   The calculator will give the answer to $15.64 \div 4.7$ as 3.327 65... but an answer given to the nearest whole number is sufficient. Therefore, $15.64 \div 4.7$ is approximately 3

5. With 52 children, 6 members of staff are required ($52 \div 10 = 5.2$ and so there must be 6, not 5, members of staff). So, $52 + 6 = 58$, say 60 people. So, need 3 minibuses. This will cost about $£100 \times 3 = £300$. If we round £6.45 to £6.50, then the tickets cost between $60 \times £6$ and $60 \times £7$, so between £360 and £420, say £400. So total cost is about $400 + 300 = £700$. (Real cost $= 60 \times £6.45 + 3 \times £98 = £681$)

6. The shortest distance is 159.5 km because 159.5 is the smallest number that would round to 160. The furthest apart they could be is a more difficult question. You probably wrote something like 160.499... or $160.4\dot{9}$ (note the dot over the 9 to show that it is a recurring decimal) and you are essentially correct. However, the answer is 160.5, even though 160.5 would round up to 161. This is because, mathematically, $160.4\dot{9} = 160.5$. If you don't think that can be true, can you write down a number that lies between $160.4\dot{9}$ and 160.5? There is no such number, so $160.4\dot{9}$ must equal 160.5.

7. 15.300 °C

8. (a) 19 000 m or 19 km   (b) $19 \div 1.6 = 11.875$ so just under 12 miles.

9. 1234×1234 must be bigger than $1000 \times 1000 = 1\,000\,000$.

   151 782 is smaller than 1 000 000 so the answer is incorrect. (Note: Eli should know that if you multiply two numbers together when both numbers have a unit digit of 4 the answer must end in 6 because $4 \times 4 = 16$. The unit digit of this answer is 4.

10. (d) 640 000 mm² would mean that the garden has length and width about 800 mm (assuming it is square), i.e. length and width both equal 80 cm. This is less than 1 m, so much too small for a garden.

    Other answers could be from 7 m × 7 m, 20 m × 20 m or 800 cm × 800 cm (8 m × 8 m), which are all sensible sizes for a garden.

11. There are about 65 million people in the UK. Primary schools cover six years; life expectancy is about 80, so about $6 \times 65 \div 80$ million $= 4.875$ million children of primary age. Say 5 million. What is the average size of a primary school? One form entry with 30 pupils per class would give 180. Two form

entry would give 360. So let's say 270 is average. 4 875 000 ÷ 270 = 18 055.5... so a reasonable estimate would be 18 000 primary schools. (In 2018/19 there were actually 20 832 primary schools in the UK, so this is not a bad estimate.)

12. This will vary from person to person. You need to define what you are including in 'television' – it would be sensible to include some things you watch on your phone or tablet or other computer, but maybe not everything. Start with how much you watch per day (or week) now and multiply up to a year. You might want to adjust for different periods of your life when you expect to watch more or less television. Average life expectancy is about 80 years.

CHAPTER 15: REPRESENTING AND INTERPRETING DATA

1. Mean = $(12 + 5 + 6 + 12 + 10 + 11 + 12 + 6 + 9 + 15) ÷ 10 = 9.8$

   Median = 10.5 (order data: 5 6 6 9 **10 11** 12 12 12 15; $(10 + 11) ÷ 2 = 10.5$)

   Mode = 12

2. (a) True

   (b) Not enough information – the charts show the proportion of time, not the length of time; we have no idea how long he spent on either.

   (c) Not enough information – this would be true if he spent the same total time on each device, but not if he spent 12 hours on his phone and only 4 hours on his tablet.

   (d) True

   (e) False – you cannot add percentages in this way. The percentages for both devices individually are less than 21% so the overall percentage cannot be 21% and must be between 8% and 13%.

3. For example, the graph shows that retention rates have decreased each year for each cohort.

4. The graph shows a small negative correlation between the two measures, indicating that more deprived students had lower Progress 8 scores on average. However, there are quite a few outlying values, particularly at the low end of the Progress 8 scores.

5. The vertical axis has been truncated to start at 18, giving a slightly misleading picture. The data on which the graph is based shows that average secondary class size rose from 20.1 to 21.7 between 2014 and 2018, an increase of 8% over 4 years, and in 2018 had returned to a similar value as in 2006. A different

report might have said that average class sizes rose slightly. Or that over the last 12 years, class sizes have remained relatively stable. Any of the three interpretations could be considered correct.

6. (a) About 64%

(b) 64% achieved B or better and 42% achieved A or better, so 22% achieved a grade B.

(c) The students did better in 2018. Drawing a line across the graph through 50% on the cumulative frequency scale gives the notional median grade. This is between A and B in both years but in 2018 it was slightly further towards the A grade. Similarly, drawing a line across through 75% for the UQ shows 75% of students achieved grade C or better in 2019 but in 2018 the UQ was between C and B. At the ends of the distribution (grades U, E and A*), the percentages were very similar for the two years.

7. (a) false   (b) false   (c) true   (d) true   (e) true

(f) false (Note: the median is not mid-way between the UQ and the LQ.)

8.

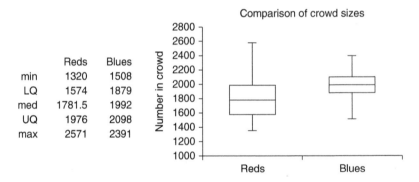

	Reds	Blues
min	1320	1508
LQ	1574	1879
med	1781.5	1992
UQ	1976	2098
max	2571	2391

So, The Blues had higher crowds on average and the sizes of their crowds were more consistent.

9. (a) Total age of 11 players is $22 \times 11 = 242$. Total age of 10 players is $10 \times 21 = 210$.

So the player sent off was $242 - 210 = 32$ years old.

(b) We are told in the question that the mean is 22, the median is 20 and the mode is 17. We also know, from part (a), that one player is 32.

_ 32 _ _ _ 20 _ _ 17   17   17

To find the maximum age, we need to make all the other players as young as possible, making sure that the maximum number of players of any age other than 17 is 2.

_ 32   21   21   20   20   18   18   17   17   17

Then to get a mean of 22, we need the total to be 242 and the oldest player must be 41.

(c) The mean and median are different so the distribution is not symmetric. This rules out A and C. Half the supporters are 20 or under and half are older than 20 but the mean is 25, so there must be some older supporters increasing the mean. So the answer is B.

10. There are many solutions to the first question, for example, 1, 1, 2, 2, 3, 4, 4, 4, 24

Smallest number is 6 boxes containing 0, 1, 2, 4, 4, 19 matches.

CHAPTER 16: PROBLEM SOLVING

1. Time in hours is $8 \div 25 = 0.32$

    $0.32 \times 60 = 19.2$ minutes. So about 20 minutes. (Note: remember that time works on a base of 60, not 10 or 100, so 0.32 does not represent 32 minutes.)

2. Total words $144 \times 170 = 24\ 480$ words $24\ 480/160 =$ about 153 minutes. 153/15 is about 10 days, so about 2 school weeks.

3. Friday 27 November

4. $135 \times 40 \div 1.463 = £3691.05$

    $3691.05 \times 1.05 = £3875.60$

5. $1.02^{10} = 1.218\ 994\ 42$ so 121.9%

6. Total words $8 \times 320 = 2560$

    1869 words already written, so 691 words left

    $691 \div 320 = 2.16$ pages, about 2 pages.

    This is about identifying the important information.

7. You need to find a way to compare the strengths.

Recipe	Ratio (fruit juice : water)	Ways to compare		
		Fraction	%	Decimal
A	5 : 4 or 1 : 0.8	$\frac{5}{9}$ or $\frac{60}{108}$	55	0.55...
B	7 : 5 or 1 : 0.7...	$\frac{7}{12}$ or $\frac{63}{108}$	58	0.58...

So B is stronger.

250 cups @ 200 ml = 50 000 ml or 50 litres

Cranberry juice is $\frac{3}{12}$ of 50 = 12.5 litres, so need 13 cartons costing 13 × 1.25 = £16.25

Orange juice is $\frac{4}{12}$ of 50 = 16.6 litres, so need 17 cartons costing 17 × 1.25 = £21.25

Water is $\frac{5}{12}$ of 50 = 20.8 litres, so 21 litres, so need 3 × 6 litres and 2 × 1.5 litres costing £8.45

250 **cups** at a cost of £1.00 for 50 will cost £2.50

Total cost = £48.45 Cost per cup = 19.38p, so charge 24 or 25p (or more).

8.

Fish		D 5 mins	G 10 mins		F 2 mins
Sauce			B 7 mins	A 3 mins	
Veg	C 4 mins		E 10 mins		

21 mins so 1.26 pm

9. (a) Could this be an age effect? Older children will have more cavities and be able to spell better (and have bigger feet).

(b) It is likely that people who are overweight drink more diet drinks to try to lose weight.

(c) It is likely that before being diagnosed with asthma, children were given antibiotics for their symptoms.

10. If there are five classes in Year 7, for example, with sizes 34, 34, 34, 12 and 6, then the median class size is 34 and the mean is 24. So, it is possible they are both correct, though unlikely as classes would probably not be structured in this way.

11. This question can be answered by working systematically through the possibilities.

The original shape is a square, so

Length of side of square (cm)	Length of sides of rectangle (cm)	Perimeter of rectangle (cm)	Area of square (cm²)
1	$1 + \frac{1}{2} + 1 + \frac{1}{2}$	3	1
2	$2 + 1 + 2 + 1$	6	4
3	$3 + 1\frac{1}{2} + 3 + 1\frac{1}{2}$	9	9
4	$4 + 2 + 4 + 2$	12	16

Or solving the problem using algebra:

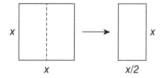

Let x cm be the length of the sides of the square. Then the dimensions of the rectangle are x, x, $\frac{x}{2}$, $\frac{x}{2}$ and the perimeter is $x + x + \frac{x}{2} + \frac{x}{2} = 3x$. This equals 12, so $x = 4$ cm and the area $= 16$ cm²

12. $4 \times \theta = 36$, so $\theta = 9$

$2 \times \theta + 2 \times \Diamond = 38$ and as $\theta = 9$ then $2 \times 9 + 2 \times \Diamond = 38$ so $\Diamond = 10$

$2 \times * + \theta + \Diamond = 43$, i.e. $2 \times * + 9 + 10 = 43$ so $2 \times * + 19 = 43$

so $2 \times * = 24$ and so $* = 12$

Therefore, row 1 = 10 + 12 + 10 + 9 = 41 and Row 4 = 10 + 12 + 12 + 10 = 44

Column 1 = 10 + 12 + 9 + 10 = 41

Column 2 = 12 + 9 + 9 + 12 = 42

Column 3 = 10 + 12 + 9 + 12 = 43

13. Length of the side of the large square = 26 cm + 24 cm + 30 cm = 70 cm

There are several ways of answering the question, for example:

Therefore: 24 + A + 8 + 24 = 70 giving A = 14 cm

So: 20 + A + B + 30 = 70, i.e. 20 + 14 + B + 30 = 70 giving B = 6 cm

$20 + A + C + 20 = 70$, i.e. $20 + 14 + C + 20 = 70$ giving $C = 16$ cm

$24 + A + D + 26 = 70$, i.e. $24 + 14 + D + 26 = 70$ giving $D = 6$ cm

14. Median must be 21 so that is the middle number. Mode is 24 so the two highest numbers must be 24. The mean is 20, so the total must be $5 \times 20 = 100$. The final two numbers must add to $100 - 24 - 24 - 21 = 31$. So, they can be any two numbers lower than 21 that sum to 31.

15. You might have solved this by trial and improvement.

    A more formal method is given here.

    Let x stand for the number of coins on the table.

    So $\dfrac{x}{2}$ is the number 'heads up'

    and $\dfrac{x}{2} - 2 = \dfrac{x}{3}$

    The common denominator is 6 so multiplying through by 6 gives:

    $\dfrac{6x}{2} - 2 \times 6 = \dfrac{6x}{3}$ which means $3x - 12 = 2x$

    Solving this equation gives $x = 12$, so 12 coins.

16. (a) The number could be: ④ ❷ total 6 or ⑤ ❽ total 13,

    or ④ ❽ total 12 or ⑤ ❷ total 7

    For parts (b), (c) and (d) a good approach is to use a grid:

    (b)

	③	⑥
❼	10	13
❿	13	16

    (c)

	②	⑤
❷	4	7
❽	10	13

    (d)

	②	⑥
❶	3	7
❺	7	11

18

GLOSSARY

SOME COMMON MATHEMATICAL TERMS AND THEIR MEANINGS

This is a list of some common mathematical terms that you may encounter in the contexts of number and data.

Term	Meaning
Accuracy	The degree of precision given in the question or required in the answer. For example, a length might be measured to the nearest centimetre, a pupil's reading age is usually given to the nearest month, the answer to a question might be given to 1 decimal place.
Average	A number used to represent the 'middle' or 'central tendency' of a data set. Common averages are the mean, median and mode.
Bar chart	A chart where the number associated with each item is shown as a horizontal or vertical bar and the length of the bar is proportional to the number it represents, for example, showing the number of times the item occurs or the value of the item being measured.

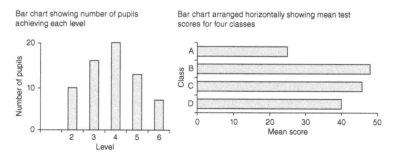

Base	Integers are usually written in base 10, using the digits: 0, 1, 2, 3, 4, 5, 6, 7, 8, 9. Numbers written, for example, in base 3 will only use the digits 0, 1, 2. In base 3 the number 25 would be written as 221 meaning 2 nines, 2 threes and 1 unit. When other bases are used, the base is given as a subscript to the last digit, so $25 = 221_3$

Billion | Nowadays the word 'billion' means a thousand million (or 10^9)

It used to mean a million million (or 10^{12}).

Box plot | Or box and whisker plot. A visual representation using the maximum, minimum and quartiles of a data set.

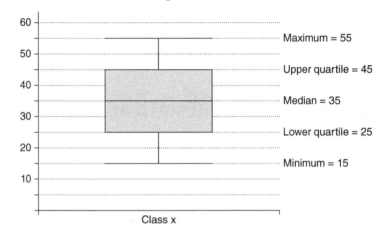

Common factor | The integers 12 and 15 both have 3 as a factor; 3 is a **common** factor of 12 and 15.

Common multiple | The integer 60 is a multiple of 12 and of 15. 60 is a **common** multiple of 12 and 15.

Consecutive | Two integers are consecutive if they differ by 1, for example 9 and 10.

Correlation | The extent to which two quantities are related. For example, there is a positive correlation between two tests, A and B, if a person with a high mark in test A is likely to have a high mark in test B and a person with a low mark in test A is likely to get a low mark in test B. A scatter graph of the two variables may help when considering whether a correlation exists between the two variables.

Cube | A cube can be

- a solid shape with 6 square faces

- a number like 64 which is $4 \times 4 \times 4 = 4^3$ or 4 cubed

Cumulative frequency | Cumulative frequency is the running total of the frequencies. On a graph, it can be represented by a cumulative frequency curve.

Decimals	Numbers based on or counted in a place value system of tens. Normally we talk about decimals when dealing with tenths, hundredths and other decimal fractions less than 1. A decimal point is placed after the units digit when writing a decimal number, e.g. 1.25.
Decimal place	In any decimal the first position after the decimal point is called the first decimal place, the second position after the decimal point is the second decimal place, and so on.
Denominator	The bottom number of a fraction.
Equation	An equation is a mathematical 'sentence' in which two numbers or expressions are linked by an '=' sign.
Expression	An expression is a collection of mathematical symbols which are added or multiplied together, subtracted or divided. For example, πr^2 is an expression for the area of a circle with radius r, and $2(l + w)$ is an expression for the perimeter of a rectangle of length l and width w.
Factor	8 is a factor of 16 because $16 = 2 \times 8$. 8 is not a factor of 20.
Formula	A formula is an equation which expresses the possible values of one variable in terms of one or more other variables. For example, $V = \pi r^2 h$ is a formula for the volume of a cylinder in terms of the radius r of the base and the height h of the cylinder.
Fraction	A number that represents a part of a whole. It consists of a numerator and a denominator. The numerator represents the number of equal parts of a whole, while the denominator is the total number of parts that make up the whole.
Frequency	The frequency of an event is the number of times the event occurs.
Frequency distribution	A list, table or graph that displays the frequency of various outcomes in a sample.
Highest common factor (HCF)	The highest common factor of two or more given integers is the largest integer which is a factor of the given integers. For example, the highest common factor of 26 and 91 is 13.
Index	When a number is written as a power, the power is called the index. For example, $1000 = 10^3$. The power '3' is called the index.

Integer	An integer is any whole number whether positive, negative or zero
Interquartile range (IQR)	A measure of variability. The upper quartile minus the lower quartile.
Lowest common multiple (LCM)	The lowest common multiple of two integers is the smallest integer which is an exact multiple of those two integers. For example, the LCM of 26 and 91 is 182.
Lowest common denominator	The lowest common denominator of two fractions is the LCM of the two denominators. For example, the lowest common denominator of $\frac{5}{26}$ and $\frac{17}{91}$ is 182. Both fractions can be written with this as denominator, $\frac{5}{26} = \frac{35}{182}$ and $\frac{17}{91} = \frac{34}{182}$ and this is the smallest such denominator.
Mean	An average calculated by adding the values and dividing the total by the number of values.
Median	An average found by ordering values and taking the middle value. When there is an even number of numbers the median is found by adding the two middle numbers and halving that total.
Mode	An average which is the most frequently occurring value.
Multiple	12 is a multiple of 3 because 3 is a factor of 12.
Non-terminating decimal	A non-terminating decimal is a decimal that goes on for ever. For example: 0.123 123 123 123... Non-terminating decimals can have a recurring block or can be non-recurring.
Numerator	The top number of a fraction. For example, in the fraction $\frac{3}{5}$ the '3' is the numerator.
Outlier	A value that is a long way from other values in a data set.
Percentage	To refer to a specific fraction of a given quantity, such as 'one-quarter of a rectangle' or 'two-thirds of a class of 30 pupils', we can express this fraction as a percentage. To calculate the percentage corresponding to a given fraction, rewrite the fraction as an equivalent fraction with a denominator of 100: the numerator of this equivalent fraction gives the percentage. For example, $\frac{1}{4} = \frac{25}{100}$ so one-quarter of a rectangle is the same as 25% of the rectangle.
Percentage points	The difference between two values, given as percentages. For example, a school has 80% attendance one year and 83% the next year. There has been an increase of 3 percentage points in attendance.

Percentiles	Values which divide the ordered data points into 100 equal parts, or percentiles.
Pie chart	A circular graph that is used to show or compare proportions.

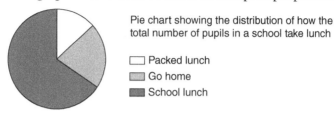

Pie chart showing the distribution of how the total number of pupils in a school take lunch

☐ Packed lunch
▨ Go home
▮ School lunch

Power	A power of 10 is a number of the form 10^2 (= 100) or 10^3 (= 1000). A power of 2 is a number like 2^0, 2^2, 2^3, ...
Product	Given a collection of two or more numbers, their product is the answer obtained when they are multiplied together.
Proportion	A number considered in comparative relation to a whole. A proportion can be expressed as a fraction, a decimal or a percentage.
Quartiles	Values which divide the ordered data points into four equal parts, or quarters.
Range	A measure of variability. The largest number in a data set minus the smallest.
Ratio	The ratio of two quantities is given by a pair of numbers separated by a colon. Here the ratio of black squares to white squares is $2:3$.

Recurring decimal	A recurring decimal is a decimal like $\frac{1}{3} = 0.333\,333\,333...$, or $\frac{1}{7} = 0.142\,857\,142\,857...$ which goes on forever repeating the same string of digits over and over.
Rounding	Expressing a number to a degree of accuracy. A number like 674 could be rounded up to 700 to the nearest hundred or down to 670 to the nearest ten. A decimal such as 123.456 can be rounded to 1 decimal place as 123.5 or rounded to 2 significant figures as 120.
Scatter diagram	Or scattergraph or scatter plot. It is a graph plotting pairs of numerical data, with one variable on each axis, to look for a relationship between them.

Sector	The part or area of a circle which is formed between two radii and the circumference. Each piece of a pie chart is a sector.
Skewed	A data set or graph is skewed if its distribution is not symmetrical.
Square	A square can be

- a 4-sided quadrilateral with all 4 sides equal in length and all 4 angles equal to 90°.

- a number like 16 which is $4 \times 4 = 4^2$ or 4 squared.

Square root	$16 = 4 \times 4$. 16 is the square of 4; 4 is the square root of 16.
Standard form	A number which is written as a number between 1 and 10 multiplied by a power of 10 is in standard form. For example, $3245 = 3.245 \times 10^3$
Statistic	A number or numerical fact which has been derived from a large set of data.
Statistics	The science of collecting and analysing numerical data.
Terminating decimal	A decimal which terminates or stops.
Time series	A data set or graph which shows how a variable has changed over time.
Trillion	10^{12} or 1 000 000 000 000

19

FURTHER RESOURCES AND REFERENCES

RESOURCES

Source	Details
BiteSize	www.bbc.com/education
CIMT [The Centre for Innovation in Mathematics Teaching]	www.cimt.org.uk
GCSE textbook(s)	Any books targeted at the Higher tier, Grade C to A* or levels 4 to 9
Khan Academy	www.khanacademy.org
Mr Barton Maths	www.mrbartonmaths.com
NCETM [National Centre for Excellence in the teaching of Mathematics]	www.ncetm.org.uk
Revision guides	e.g. GCSE AQA Mathematics Higher Level, published by CGP Books. (Note: there are similar books for other awarding bodies such as OCR and Edexcel)
STEM [Science, Technology, Engineering and Mathematics]	www.stem.org.uk

REFERENCES

Bloom, B.S. (Ed.), Engelhart, M.D., Furst, E.J., Hill, W.H., and Krathwohl, D.R. (1956). *Taxonomy of Educational Objectives: The Classification of Educational Goals. Handbook 1: Cognitive Domain.* New York: David McKay.

DfE (2011). *Teachers' Standards.* London: HMSO.

DfE (2013). *National Curriculum.* London: HMSO.

DfE (2019a, Sept.). *Initial Teacher Training Core Content Framework.* London: HMSO.

DfE (2019b). 'Reducing workload: supporting teachers in the early stages of their career. Advice for school leaders, induction tutors, mentors and appropriate bodies'. Available at: https://core.ac.uk/reader/199234376 [Accessed 11 March 2021].

DfE (2019c). *Early Career Framework.* London: HMSO.

DfE (2020a, 4 Sept.). *Initial Teacher Training (ITT): Criteria and supporting advice,* section C1.3. London: HMSO.

DfE (2020b, 27 Oct.). *School Census.* London: HMSO.

GCSE AQA Mathematics for Grade 9-1 (2016). Broughton-in-Furness: Coordination Group Publications Ltd.

Gill, T. (2018, Sept.). 'How have students and schools performed on the Progress 8 performance measure?' Paper presented at the annual conference of the British Educational Research Association, Northumbria University, Newcastle, UK.

OFSTED (2021, Jan.) 'Introduction. Guidance January 2021: Maintained schools and academies'. Available at: www.gov.uk/guidance/january-2021-maintained-schools-and-academies) [Withdrawn 16 April 2021].

ENGLISH INDEX

MATHEMATICS INDEX